"Alice Rothchild's new book is a masterpiece of the journal genre. Carefully and beautifully written, it is invaluable as an ethnography blending slices of daily life among Jews and Palestinians with exceptionally keen insights and observations about the ongoing regional tragedy. She sees and listens with the trained, sympathetic eye and ear of a physician and also of a Jew who understands that Israel can end the occupation while Palestinians cannot. Eschewing polemics altogether, she persuades by compassionately attending to the fears, angers, hopes, and wishes of a broad range of people, in effect representing the range of parties involved."

—**GORDON FELLMAN**
Professor of Sociology,
Chair, Peace, Conflict, and Coexistence Studies,
Brandeis University

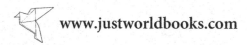

ON THE BRINK

Just World Books is an imprint of Just World Publishing, LLC.

Typesetting by Jane Sickon for Just World Publishing, LLC.

Second Printing
ISBN (pb): 978-1-935982-44-9
ISBN (e): 978-1-935982-46-3
LCCN: 2014947320

Contents

former Jerusalem bureau chief. His article is titled "A Damaging Distance." In it, he reflects on the events of the past few weeks, and then he looks back to what he sees as a better time when Palestinians worked in Israel, Israelis shopped in the West Bank and "snack[ed] on plates of unparalleled hummus," although he admits that even this human contact had a "colonial quality." I am intrigued by his presentation of an endearing and somewhat delusional Jewish self-image (we are the long suffering good people with the "most moral army in the world") and appalled by his rosy recollections of a better time and inability to see the larger context of this struggle. Since when was colonialism something desirable on which to reminisce?

For me, sitting here in my home near Boston, Massachusetts, I feel like I am living in several clashing universes. I grew up in a Jewish family with a deep love of Israel and a profound understanding of the horrors of the Holocaust and the need for Jews to be "safe," but I have come to see the past and the present through a lens that painfully clashes with many of the founding mythologies of the State of Israel.

Now, I have just returned from three weeks of travelling in Israel and the West Bank. I was making this trip partly on my own and partly with a fact-finding delegation organized by the Health and Human Rights Project of American Jews for a Just Peace and Jewish Voice for Peace Boston. This is the tenth such delegation I have been on in the past eleven years. In addition to investigating and trying to understand the health status of Palestinians and Israelis, these delegations also express our solidarity with Jewish and Palestinian activists working on the ground in a host of different settings.

We visited mixed cities in Israel where the implications of an inherently racist society that benefits Jews over all other citizens is flagrantly obvious if you only stop to look. We visited cities and villages in the West Bank where decades of occupation and checkpoints and permits and a ballooning Jewish settler population have strangled the Palestinian people. We would have visited medical colleagues and friends inside Gaza but permits have long been near impossible to obtain. We arrived during the longest hunger strike by Palestinian prisoners, many of them political activists mostly in administrative detention. We then watched with fear and horror when the three yeshiva students from Hebron disappeared; and we witnessed the provocative massive increase in Israeli Defense Force (IDF) incursions and arrests in the West Bank, despite the lack of evidence as to the identity of the murderers. I left the day the students' bodies were "found," although I later learned that the IDF had known the settler teens were dead shortly after the murders but covered up that information to create a justification for a major incursion into the West Bank to "search" for them. The gruesome revenge killing of a Palestinian boy, the beating of the Palestinian American teenager, the rampages of racist Jewish thugs attacking everything Arab in Israeli cities, East Jerusalem and the West Bank, the appalling rants on social media, the rockets (Hamas and otherwise), the F-16s bombing Gaza: all that happened during the first two weeks I was home, trying to grapple with all of this out-of-control insanity.

It is painfully clear to me that the events of the last few weeks did not happen in a vacuum, that the occupation of the West Bank and the siege of Gaza, the growing Jewish settlements in the West Bank, the increasingly racist right-wing governments in Israel, and the very idea that Jewish suffering and Jewish exceptionalism gives "us" the right to eliminate or oppress another people, created the environment for this explosion. This is not about the last ten or twenty years, this is about the very unsettling consequences of Zionism itself. It is also clear to me, a committed pacifist and social justice advocate, that the ongoing Palestinian resistance (mostly, thankfully, nonviolent), is actually something that I feel compelled to support, while rejecting all violence, state sponsored and otherwise. I do not do this out of an undying love for Palestinians or any dislike of my fellow-Jews (the "self-hating Jew" accusation that is so frequently thrown at people like me.) I do this because I have learned that Jews are capable of the same racism, hatred, and atrocities as anyone else. I do this because we must be held accountable for our actions and our beliefs. I do this because not doing this makes us monsters who have lost all sense of moral compass.

I have come to these conclusions by witnessing the facts on the ground, asking difficult questions, challenging myself beyond my comfort zones and yes, seeing myself in the eyes of my so-called enemy. I invite you to walk with me on this challenging and empowering journey to a more honest place, where the potential for lasting political and social change is grounded in our common humanity and the recognition of injustices wherever and to whom-ever they may fall.

Members of American Jews for a Just Peace, Health and Human Rights Project, June 2014, gather at the historic clock tower in Nablus, West Bank.

June 12, 2014

"Welcome to Israel, Bien Venue"

I often encounter some metaphorical weirdness on my flights to Israel, and, true to form, on my layover in Toronto, my flight leaves from gate E69, but arrows point in opposite directions and the obvious glass doors to the indicated area are locked shut. Alice in Wonderland? Where is the white rabbit when I need him? A helpful information lady explains that *that* section of the airport is locked until shortly before check-in. Ahhhh. I settle into an anxious, watchful stupor, and once the doors open, I notice that E69 is also cordoned off and that another (mild Canadian style, sweep of the wand across my potentially explosive laden palms) checkpoint is required to enter the now safe-from-terror zone that is the flight to Tel Aviv.

The passengers are an eclectic group: a number of Christian religious tours, gold crosses draped around necks, tee shirts quoting Isaiah and scripture, a "Walk with the Bible" group, folks on the "Jesus Trail," lots of prayer and blessings in general conversation, a large unnaturally enthusiastic Taglit Birthright-Israel team complete with name tags and youthful happiness, eager to fall in love with the great Zionist outdoors. Families wearing yarmulkes, kids alternating "Daddy" and "Abba," tee shirts in Hebrew, a woman in a hijab with five children, a man with thick grey hair reading a Russian newspaper.

Eleven plus hours later, at passport control, the lines are full, hot, sweaty and slow moving. A family from the United States behind me is coming for a wedding. The father is insisting that Israel is an egalitarian society and his determined teenage daughter argues intently that he is indeed wrong. There is a bank of security devices all made by Hewlett Packard, a US company. Two little Chinese ladies in big hats chat with another Asian woman on yet another

Christian holy sites tour. They are inexplicably turned away from passport control and led away to some unnamed place. I watch my passport official carefully; she takes her job seriously, asks lots of questions, and is constantly on the phone. An ominous sign for me. I review my spiel: nice Jewish lady, loves Israel, meeting friend who speaks Hebrew, plus check out my last name. *Rothchild*. It seems to me that almost everyone sweating in the foreign passport queue is on some kind of pilgrimage: looking for Jesus, or for a love of Zion and a tan muscular Israeli soldier to play with in the great outdoors, or for family connections; and then there is me, looking for the contradictions in this booming, high tech, flawed, complicated so-called democracy.

I am trying to resist stereotypes, but as I board the *sherut* (the shared taxi to Jerusalem), the bulky probably Russian driver and an elderly Orthodox Jewish woman begin what appears to be a pretty intense argument with loud, angry yelling. She is soon joined by her bearded husband in a long dark coat and yarmulke, wearing wire rimmed glasses, and this noisy argument continues for a good fifteen minutes into the drive. What happened to civility and "using inside voices," as I used to tell my children? (My slightly sleep deprived fantasy is that he does not want to sit next to a strange woman, and I have already decided to take a moral stand: I will not give up my single seat, but that apparently was not the issue. My paranoia relaxes, but the tension in the van is still palpable.) I can feel this peculiar cultural insanity creeping into my pores. Shortly thereafter, the couple begins chatting (loud but friendly) with another older man in a mix of Hebrew and Yiddish. It seems all the personality disorders are now under control.

The heat is thick and there is a haze over the landscape; tall cities cluster like stark giant grey Legos, the fields and hills are turning from green to straw-brown. We turn onto Highway 443, past Modi'in, acres of Jewish National Fund pine forests (often covering destroyed Palestinian villages), young Israeli soldiers wait at bus stops, gigantic cranes and concrete cities mushroom everywhere. We are soon on the segment that it is actually in the West Bank (does anyone else in the *sherut* know this???) The metal fencing begins; Palestinian houses in the distance have black water tanks on their roofs due to the erratic water supply; looming grey Israeli guard towers flash by. The ancient hills are terraced, bleak and magnificent; rugged, graceful olive trees hug the soil. The separation wall is now concrete, there is more rolling barbed wire. We stop briefly at an Israeli checkpoint and then are waved through. I guess we passed the ethnic profiling test. I see an ominous grey prison just near the turn off to Ramallah, probably Ofer Prison. I think of all the Palestinian hunger strikers protesting in Israeli jails. The walls along the highway are now turning more picturesque, patterned brick designs (making the occupation pretty?) and then more imposing concrete as we near the Holy City.

We return to Highway 1 and head into Jerusalem and begin a brief tour of the Jewish settlements. The two older "yellers" are met in Ramat Shlomo by their happy family and four grandchildren, all modestly attired. They leave their Yiddish buddy with a friendly "*Yalla*," which is Arabic for "Let's go." We are then off to the Jewish settlements of Pisgat Ze'ev and French Hill, a former Arab neighborhood, an older Orthodox man shouts at a car that has stopped in the cross walk, gesturing fitfully. We pass the refugee camp of Shuafat. More opaque walls. I watch with my x-ray vision, all the history, the conflict, the players, the demons are all here in living color, if one only stops to look. Is anyone looking?

Disneyfication of the Old City

The *sherut* drops me in front of the dusty Jerusalem Hotel, a former Arab mansion, where I stop for a bottle of water and a deep breath. A breeze wafts through the grape vines that cover the outdoor restaurant and the smell of sweet tobacco and soft conversation calm my exhausted brain. The #21 bus to Bethlehem is a few blocks around the corner, through dusty construction and open markets, across from Damascus Gate and the grey-cream walls of the Old City. A woman helps me with my bag, everyone says "*Sli ha*" (pardon my Hebrew transliteration of "excuse me"), and young men repeatedly give up their seats for older women. The bus driver stops for a late passenger and opens the door. Folks talk in a low hum and Arabic music pulses from the radio. Forgive my stereotyping *again*, but I feel a sense of respectfulness and basic decency towards each person. The lady sitting next to me and my pile of backpacks and computer case works as a cook in Jerusalem and commutes from Beit Jala every day. She asks how can she help me (I surmise that I look like someone who needs help) and offers me a candy. We pass signs for the City of David where a massive highly politicized archeological excavation and park development is underway, designed to prove that the Jews were here first and thus can toss out the several thousand years of subsequent ownership and history. We pass Silwan and Sheikh Jarrah where there is an active program to dispossess the local Palestinians and turn property over to right-wing Jewish settlers. As the bus fills to standing room only, my new friend points out a tunnel which goes under a no-man's land, she explains, between Arab and Jew. I notice a new, somewhat more ominous version of the separation wall, large concrete panels with vertical elements that meet another wall extending out at an angle, clearly constructed to deflect thrown objects or humans attempting to scale the barrier.

I am met by a friend outside of Deheisha Refugee Camp in Bethlehem where he is working on a three-year project titled Builders of Peace, funded by the European Union and organized by the Lagee Center in Aida Camp. He is working with seventy-two college students all over the West Bank and they are now discussing issues of identity and memory. He is showing my documentary film, Voices Across the Divide (www.voicesacrossthedivide. com), which tells the Israel/Palestine conflict through the stories of Palestinians living in the United States. This is complicated on so many levels and I am both humbled and excited. The screening at the camp is met with lively conversations and many questions about the motivations and messages of an American Jew. I cannot blame them.

We head to the village of Al Walaja, a small town northwest of Bethlehem located on the seam zone where there is an active struggle over the separation wall and the continuing loss of land in the shadows of the Jewish settlements of Gilo and Har Gilo. In a small community center, as eleven students listen politely, I am washed with a sense of amazement and wonder that my documentary (with Arabic subtitles), carefully designed for US audiences, has made its way to this remote and resilient place; of what use could it possibly be? How will the students feel about a Jewish woman presenting their story? Have they heard their own histories or has that been swallowed in the memories of the traumatized and the Israeli occupation? I am relieved to hear that the students are well versed in history; two are upset that I refer to the war in 1948 as a "civil war," as that implies to them that the Jewish immigrants have an equal claim to Historic Palestine as have indigenous Palestinians. They all want to know what is my message? How do I describe Israel? We talk and talk. I am glad I have come.

I return to East Jerusalem that evening in a car with Israeli plates rented in East Jerusalem by the Palestinian American wife of my friend who is working on the EU project. She also has Israeli citizenship through her father, who is an Israeli Palestinian, but she spends the summers with her husband's family in the Aida refugee camp in Bethlehem. We are stopped at a checkpoint, two white-appearing ladies, maybe Jewish, who knows? Middle aged. Yellow plates, that's kosher, and we're waved through. I always forget the intensity of ethnic profiling in these parts.

Instead of a quick trip, we are soon stuck in massive amounts of barely crawling traffic; it seems that tonight is part of the festival of lights in Jerusalem. There are all sorts of gaudy, sparkly, twinkly light sculptures and over-the-top multicolored light displays, but I am completely appalled by the light show projected on the magnificent, ancient Damascus gate and the stone walls on each side that surround the Old City—supposedly a hotly contested, ancient, sacred site to the three Abrahamic religions. To the accompaniment of rousing movie score music, the stones are bathed in multicolored displays, covered with Persian (i.e., Iranian) tapestries, large eyes blink and hands move turrets, curtains sweep open, the walls are striped, plaid, bathed in flames, water, cobwebs, ancient figures, and monumental machinery, a massive gyration mishmash of bad Disney movies: *Arabian Nights* meets *The Little Mermaid*, *Cinderella*, *My Little Pony*, and *The Lion King*. It is awesome and awful, tacky and tasteless. I am too amazed and sleep deprived to wrap my brain around this (fanatic Jewish settlers are plotting to blow up Al Aqsa Mosque and build the third temple while a tacky Hollywood display cheapens the entire place? Really?) and I head off on the cobbled stones and dark alleys to the Via Dolorosa and the Austrian Hospice where a clean bunk bed and a large cross on the wall await me. I fantasize that I am joining a convent and this is only the beginning of a life of simplicity and austerity when sleep finally sweeps me away into the land of official insanity.

Well-armed Israeli Defense Forces and other Israeli security are visible in Israeli cities and in the West Bank. Here, two soldiers stand outside the Damascus Gate in the Old City of Jerusalem, making their presence felt among an unarmed civilian population.

June 13, 2014

The Social and Political Determinants of Health Care: i.e. Don't get Sick While Palestinian

So this is my current understanding of a fragment of Palestinian health care (take a deep breath and suspend any concepts you may harbor regarding the right to health):

A Palestinian family calls an ambulance in East Jerusalem; the call goes to the Magen David Adom (Israeli ambulance service, which is, by the way, bound by international agreements). If the MDA determines that this is a "high risk" neighborhood, they demand a police escort and will not enter the area until the police arrive. The (Palestinian) Red Crescent ambulance (they are not allowed to use "Palestinian" in their title in East Jerusalem and are also tracked by GPS) can also be called directly but that is a different not-so-well known number. If the police do not come, then the Red Crescent is called, but if the situation is determined to be too dangerous, depending on the location, the Palestinian Medical Relief Society (PMRS) ambulance is called.

But PMRS ambulances are based in Al Bireh in the West Bank and must pass through checkpoints and inspections and cannot reliably enter East Jerusalem. Palestinian ambulance drivers must have permits to drive the ambulance and personal permits to enter East Jerusalem; the permits last six months and they are often given with dates that do not entirely overlap, so there are months when the drivers are unable to work. Palestinians in need of critical care from the West Bank face huge barriers, often have to *walk* (okay, imagine chest pain, leg fracture, bleeding wound, emaciation and weakness from cancer, and *walking*) across checkpoints or be transferred by gurney between two back-to-back ambulances at a checkpoint. (I have seen this with vegetable produce—it can ruin a shipment of tomatoes—but human beings?) A Palestinian living in East Jerusalem is covered under Israeli insurance, which does not pay for the Red Crescent ambulance which is often the only one that is able to come, thus the ailing patient (should he or she survive) is also out 150 shekels for the crime of being sick while Palestinian in a racist society.

Ambulances get to Jewish Israelis in an average of seven minutes.

In the case of a motor vehicle accident in the West Bank, ambulance pick-up is determined by the *identity* of each victim: Magen David transports the Jews (i.e., settlers); Palestinian Red Crescent transports the Christian and Muslim Palestinians. (The unaffiliated I suppose are clearly out of luck.) But if the doctor determines that the Palestinian needs high level care that is only offered in East Jerusalem, the patient is transported to Qalandia checkpoint, where a "humanitarian line" is intermittently open, there are huge traffic jams, and an East Jerusalem ambulance is supposed to meet the patient there for a back-to-back transfer, if appropriate permits are obtained which are ultimately determined by the Shin Bet, the Israeli General Security Services.

These medical decisions are reportedly made by the Israeli health coordinator, Dalia Basa, an Iraqi Jew who speaks some Arabic, has worked in the West Bank since the 1970s, and holds immense power around issues of patient permits. There is another COGAT (Coordinator of Government Activities in the Territories), which is, by the way, under the Ministry of Defense, for the Erez checkpoint in Gaza. The barriers to obtaining permits also include lack of phone availability, inadequate communication with Israeli hospitals, broken fax machines, the moods of young IDF soldiers or privately hired security guards (sometimes referred to as thugs) at checkpoints who are the ultimate arbiters of passage and who sometimes do security checks (even on ambulances and UN cars, which is illegal) and sometimes don't. I am told that these eighteen to twenty-one year olds with large guns and no medical knowledge decide if a case is medically "severe": Is there blood? Burns? Is the woman in labor or just "fat"? The sister of a friend, in labor with a real pregnancy, when faced with the obstacles at the checkpoint to Jerusalem, just gave up, turned around, and delivered in Ramallah rather than face the risk of a dangerous checkpoint delivery.

Forgive me if I sound angry. It is stunning what one can learn just listening to health care providers and administrators chatting over a cup of thick Arabic coffee in an office in East Jerusalem. There are so many injustices, some imposed by occupation, racism, and fear, and some by internal dysfunction. There is a growing drug problem in East Jerusalem (think poverty, hopelessness, no police protection or functional court system, and dealers running out of an Israeli crime network), currently mostly young men on heroin, and there are three small NGOs working on drug rehabilitation. Abu Dis (a neighborhood of East Jerusalem divided by the separation wall) just developed its *first* forensic center and one is just now developing in Ramallah, so solving crimes is still a bit of a mystery.

East Jerusalemites pay the same taxes as West Jerusalemites and get minimal to no municipal services. There is not enough garbage collection, few playgrounds, and, until two months ago, Palestinians did not even have addresses! There are now apartment numbers and street names, but they are not the names that people have used for years, and everyone has a post office box anyway. In Beit Hanina, a neighborhood in East Jerusalem, the water supply is connected to Ramallah but the sewer is connected to the Israeli system. Recently residents were hit with a bill for seven years of sewer service charges. The municipality charges an occupancy tax (Arnona) which is based on the size of the houses. Arab homes tend to be bigger, housing large extended families; Jewish Israeli houses tend to be smaller, more urban. As a consequence Arab families have been penalized with greater taxes since 1967. As one public health worker noted, "This causes hypertension." I wonder if this qualifies as torture by sheer constant aggravation.

The Association for Civil Rights in Israel recently documented the absence of mental health clinics in East Jerusalem, and there was also a petition about the inadequate number of post offices in East Jerusalem. These deficiencies do not happen by accident. One woman involved in health advocacy noted, as Jerusalem (and Israel as well with its expanding ultra-Orthodox population and steady flight of the alienated and disenchanted) grows more traditional, more tribal and family based, both for Jews and Palestinians, patriarchy grows stronger and women pay the price. There is a "de-modernizing influence," a constriction of the space in which women can breathe, grow, and explore. When civil law does not adequately protect the population, people turn to social family law. I see so many ramifications to these distressing trends, from the health of the individual to the health of the overall society.

And in case you forgot:

> **Geneva Convention IV, Article 56:**
> The occupying power has the duty of ensuring and maintaining with the cooperation of national and local authorities, the medical and hospital establishments and services, public health and hygiene in the occupied territory... Medical personnel of all categories shall be allowed to carry out their duties.

> **International Human Rights Law:**
> The Right to Health is composed of four essential, inter-related elements (1) Availability; (2) Accessibility, both physical and financial; (3) Acceptability; and (4) Quality.
>
> CESCR, General Comment No. 14

Where do we begin?

June 14, 2014

A Blurring of Boundaries and Conscience

I have been on a number of tours of Jerusalem with staff from the Israeli Committee Against House Demolitions (ICAHD) and I never cease to feel this wave of disbelief, shock, and deepening horror. Chaska Katz, a high energy thirty-something from a progressive, apolitical family ("my parents were hippies") came of age in the small circles of the Israel left, refused to serve in the army, started agitating for animal rights, and ultimately found her way to defending the rights of migrants, refugees, and Palestinians. ICAHD's focus on fighting Palestinian home demolitions provides her with a concrete nonviolent activity that is often a symbolic resistance but sometimes produces life-changing results. She is fluent in English, Hebrew, and Arabic.

We leave the Old City on Hebron Road towards the Jewish settlement of Talpiot and gather on a lookout in the neighborhood of Jabal al Mukabbir. In stifling heat, to our far left we can see West Jerusalem, characterized by tall high rises, apartments, hotels, fourteen huge cranes, swaths of green, parks, gardens; a constantly expanding city pushing its boundaries with massive construction. A Jewish success story! The cranes represent not only high rises, but also an exploding public infrastructure: highways, bridges, tunnels, solid "facts on the ground," i.e., THIS BELONGS TO US.

My eye moves east to the Old City with the gleaming gold dome and two adjacent crowded Palestinian villages cascading down the hill, Silwan and Wadi Joz (dotted with recent Jewish settler homes), and then further east, the scattered grey-white Palestinian houses topped by black water towers, now tending to vertical growth as there are no legal places to spread horizontally. The contrasts are stark: no parks, no green space, no cranes, empty patches of barren dry hills. Remember, these folks pay the same city taxes as the happy Jews in West Jerusalem with their sidewalks and garbage collection and street lights. More than half of the Palestinians in East Jerusalem have no sewerage or water connection and often tap into existing pipes, thus dropping the water pressure. Mekrot, the Israeli water company, refuses to lay more pipe, and many Palestinians have no water two to three days per week. I see a Palestinian boy biking in small circles on his roof, another on a swing, rocking back and forth, also on a roof. Those are obviously their playgrounds. Because there is no garbage collection, Palestinians burn their garbage, so these little boys are playing in air that is directly polluted by the neglect and racism of Israeli authorities. The numbers are stark. The Jerusalem municipal budget allots 8–10% of its finances to one-third of its population.

On a more distant hill is the Mount of Olives and the tower of Augusta Victoria Hospital, a major tertiary care hospital in East Jerusalem, and then to the southeast, the neighborhoods of Abu Dis and Azaria, now separated from Jerusalem by the eight to ten meter high concrete separation wall, cutting through the fabric of life and community and its access to the holy sites and medical care of East Jerusalem.

Further in the distance is the expansive Jewish settlement of Ma'ale Adumim, stretching its borders eastward to Jericho with the hope of ultimately bisecting the West Bank.

Intellectually I know all of this, but the visual reality is breathtaking. Chaska reviews the history of 1948, 1967, the various displacements of Jews and Palestinians during the wars, and the ultimate annexation of Jerusalem as the "undivided capital of Israel." (So much for the two-state solution, FYI.) She explains that for Palestinians to maintain their treasured East Jerusalem ID, they have to constantly prove that East Jerusalem is the center of their life and work, and this requirement creates enormous hardship. There was a massive panicked influx of East Jerusalemites living in suburbs like Hizmeh and Abu Dis when the wall was built and they feared getting stuck on the wrong side. Study abroad? Risk losing your ID. Work in Ramallah because there is no work at home? Risk losing your ID. Build a house just across from the wall because your eight children are now married and having children and there is no place to build and permits are impossible? Risk losing your ID. And the list goes on. I often feel that Israeli authorities are ethnically cleansing East Jerusalem one Palestinian at a time.

A new piece of information for me is that 60 to 80% of the land seized in Jerusalem in 1948 was Palestinian agricultural land. Even more was taken after 1967, so that Palestinians have continuously lost their source of income and employment and have migrated in large numbers into the cities, providing Israel with a source of cheap, easily exploited labor. (Remember Israeli labor laws do not apply to these folks.) And now (after the intifadas) this exploited labor has returned to the Israeli labor market by the tens of thousands, cleaning the streets, planting the gardens, building the roads and apartments that only displace them further.

With Oslo in 1993, the rapid growth of Jewish settlements in Palestinian neighborhoods began in earnest, as did the Judaization of East Jerusalem and its ever-expanding boundaries. I found it helpful to understand that Jerusalem actually has three boundaries:

1. The 1967 Municipal boundary includes East Jerusalem; Palestinians with East Jerusalem IDs must live only in East Jerusalem.
2. Greater Jerusalem includes the settlement blocks of Giv'at Ze'ev in the north, Ma'ale Adumim in the east, and Gush Etzion in the south forming a giant Jewish ring around East Jerusalem.
3. Metropolitan Jerusalem was approved in 1995 and includes Ramallah (!!!), Bethlehem (!!!) and Beit Shemesh. This boundary is about zoning, development, and, of course, ultimately settlement growth.

The net effect is that Palestinian neighborhoods as well as cities are surrounded and constricted by growing Jewish settlements and thus unable to expand; each settlement brings with it an infrastructure of bypass roads and military bases. Palestinian freedom of movement is even further eroded, and the areas of Palestinian life are thus reduced to isolated enclaves. Coming here year after year, I am bearing witness to this crushing reality.

Similar patterns exist within East Jerusalem, where the Palestinian population has grown from 66,000 in 1967 to 300,000 in 2013, but only 13% of the land is zoned for residential use and no new Palestinian neighborhoods have been built. This contrasts to the 52% of the land that is green zoned, i.e., for open space, infrastructure, and ultimately Jewish settlements. This is in addition to the 35% of East Jerusalem already zoned for Jewish settlement development. Apartheid anyone?

This is a long and myth-shattering tour. We visit the Jewish settlement of Ma'ale Zeiteim, built by the US doctor and casino magnate Irving Moskowitz. During the Shalit negotiations, the settlement hosted two large banners: "Kahani was right! Death to the Arabs!" and "One Jew equals 1,000 Arabs." I look at the manicured lawns, the recycling bins, the lovely baby carriages, and the flowers blooming in charming gardens planted in this desert community. And of course the security cameras, the guards, and I remember that this place is actually a bunker overlooking the angry residents of Ras al 'Amud. There are more settlements like this strategically dotting the hills, and gradually the pieces are coming together, the segments of wall are linking up, the massive prison for Judea and Samaria is completed. Palestinian villages like Beit Iksa and Biddu are trapped in tiny enclaves, surrounded by loops of wall, isolated from their communities. Some like Anata and Shuafat have residents with East Jerusalem IDs who just ended up on the wrong side of history. Some villages now are devoid of any services and are basically lawless areas with drugs and arms trafficking and no police force. The bureaucracy of occupation is in full force and it is mean-spirited and physically destructive. Meanwhile the permitting system in the West Bank has become more severe, there are increasing physical, social, and emotional barriers, more collaborators drawn from the ranks of the young, the frightened, the desperate.

I peer over the ridge into a deep blue artificial lake built at the base of a hill in Ma'ale Adumim and learn of the three Olympic-size swimming pools; I marvel at the series of rotaries graced by thousand-year-old olive trees uprooted from some ancient village that probably does not have a regular water supply. I remember the poverty stricken Jahalin Bedouin encampments off the highway leading to this paradise in the desert. I think of the nightmare permitting process for a Palestinian who wants to expand his house and has to prove that it is part of some master plan (there are none) and that there is proof of ownership by Israeli standards (never mind the land deed from the Ottoman Empire and the generations of family who have lived there). And then there are the demolition orders, and the legal maneuvers, and the bulldozer in the middle of the night with the fully armed soldiers, and the helicopters overhead, and the rubble and screaming children, and then of course the fine and the bill for demolition. Half of suicide bombers experienced their homes demolished as children. Trauma, hopelessness, rage anyone?

I wonder: What kind of society have we become? What kind of people do this to each other, then kiss their children and sleep without nightmares? Do the nice Hadassah ladies, the American tourists having a spiritual moment on the Via Dolorosa, the sunburned Birthright teens playing frisbee on a Tel Aviv beach care? What are the ugly consequences of grabbing everything over and over again and then only wanting more?

June 15, 2014

To Exist Is to Resist:
Challenging the Occupied Mind

Today our health and human rights delegation of nine energetic women in various states of jet lag is about to encounter walls: the kind that occupy minds, create concrete barriers, instigate wars, enhance legal institutions, and undergird international accords. In Ramallah, Mahmoud Nawajaa, from the organization Stop the Wall, takes us through a speedy overview of the last one hundred years of Palestinian history. While much was familiar (see my blog entries online from 2013), the bits and pieces that struck my frazzled brain include:

1. The 1948 war resulted in the expulsion of 45% of the indigenous Palestinian population.
2. The Herzliya Conference in Israel which started in 2000 laid the foundations for the development of the Galilee, the development of the Negev, the expansion of Greater Jerusalem, and the disengagement plans for the West Bank and Gaza. What is happening now is all part of a greater plan; little happens by accident.
3. As places like Tel Aviv become increasingly gentrified and expensive, there is a strong motivation to move into the Jewish settlements in the West Bank where much housing is free or subsidized and the environment is less crowded, and thus we are seeing this steady population shift into the occupied territories by Jewish Israelis who think they are moving east to live in a nice Israeli suburb.

4. Before 1967, Palestinians had a strong, growing economy with an agricultural industry in the north, a touristic and pilgrim industry in the center, dairy and grape production in the south, a strong cross-border trade, food-processing industries in the West Bank and Gaza, and minerals from the Dead Sea. This has all been effectively destroyed by Israeli occupation and military incursions and the severe restrictions with which we are now familiar.

5. The Palestinian Authority, the Israeli government, and international groups cooperate on creating industrial zones in the West Bank in Jenin, Hebron, and Jericho and in Gaza and on developing border industrial zones and agro-industrial zones in the Jordan Valley that do not comply with Israeli labor and environmental laws.

6. Palestinian women play a major force in the resistance and often protect male protestors, putting their bodies between their men and the Israeli soldiers.

7. Youth resistance is the vision for future political change.

But there is nothing like walking in the dust and rubble of reality and we are soon off for a tour of Qalqilya, the first walled city in the West Bank. We rumble by clusters of yellow taxis, incessant honking, and blasts of music; past the Muqataa where Arafat was once humiliated by Israeli troops and is now memorialized in grand fashion. There are pyramids of watermelons, and dark melons mounted on upside down cans, looking like rows of canons. I spot signs for Rawabi, the new city being built for locals by a Palestinian developer with shady connections whose general counsel is Dov Weissglass, the Israeli official who famously said: "The idea is to put the Palestinians on a diet, but not to make them die of hunger." The highway to the city is being built in Area C (Israeli control), funding is from the Palestinian Authority and a Qatari real estate firm, partnering with the PA, the land was bought out from Palestinian farmers and olive growers who have lived there for generations. Rumors are that the apartments will be for returning refugees (who are obviously not from Rawabi because it is new), but the condo prices are out of reach for even some Ramallah yuppies. The Jewish

National Fund has generously contributed one thousand trees. With friends like these...

While we are hurtling along at over sixty miles per hour on winding hilly roads, I try translating the environment around me. Coils of barbed wire, look for a nearby settlement or military road. I see the large sign for the Jewish settlement of Halamish and a tiny sign for the village of Nabi Saleh, which is engaged in a bitter struggle over lost land and water. The barren, concrete high rises of Rawabi erupt on a hill surrounded by cranes, while small Palestinian villages with pointy minarets and mosques, surrounded by gorgeous rocky hills, terraces, olive groves, children running along the road, donkeys braying, feel at one with the ancient landscape. The word organic comes to mind. Straight, well-paved bypass highways with lights and guard rails lord over us as we zoom through the tunnels below, countless Jewish settlements pop by, Kirya Netafim, Azzun, etc., cluster on high places.

Suhad Hashem, the guide from the Palestinian Medical Relief Society in Qalqilya, is in a rush; the farmer's gate is only open from one to two p.m. and we are late. We now enter the alternative reality of occupation. There are rows of trucks, open carts, bedraggled horses and donkey-drawn carts, and mostly resigned farmers and young boys waiting. Barbed wire curls in each direction and the main gate is opened only for vehicles and carts after permits (for human and beast or vehicle) are checked. A smaller gate to the left is for the townspeople whose farmlands are beyond the walls. They negotiate lines, a turnstile, and a security clearance every day, coming and going. Suhad notes, "I hate this a lot, I can see my father's land and aquifer, but I can never get there. I have been doing tours since 2004." Her eyes look teary. Turning around I can see the Jewish settlement of Alfe Menashe spreading across the landscape. Everything is up close and really personal. The Israeli soldiers manning the gates are dressed for mortal combat.

At another point, Suhad points to the settlement of Mattan, which has crept across the green line onto private Palestinian land which is now green and flourishing with the stolen water as well. They also have a tall security tower looking down on Qalqilya. We meet with a farmer who once had one of the largest nurseries in the area and admire the long rows of fruit and olive trees and hear his story of land loss at the hands of the bypass road. The rest of

his land is on the other side of the highway, which requires permits and planning; it is hard to find workers willing to put up with
this hassle. He says with a bit of a twinkle in his eye and a brown,
weathered face, "Even if you have your land, you can't be sure of
everything." His two sons have gone to medical school; he does not
know what the future will hold.

We return to Suhad's office where she talks about her work with
Al Mubadara, the democracy movement headed by Dr. Mustafa
Barghouti. Suhad works to improve women's conditions in sewing factories, challenging low wages and long hours, as well as to
improve their access to health screenings. She is also active in the
schools, urging students to boycott Israeli products. "Each shekel
comes back to us as bullets or settlements" and "Don't buy from
the occupier."

She explains that Qalqilyians have lost so much land that they
are considered as refugees and receive services from the United
Nations with UNRWA schools and hospitals. They are also located
on the largest water aquifer in the West Bank. She talks about the
towns caught between loops of wall and the green line, which are
not recognized, have no services, and are not even allowed to bury
their dead. She talks about the settlers from nearby Azun Atma
who refuse to ride on buses with Palestinian workers. Her daughter
is studying swimming training for women at Najah University in
Nablus.

We head back outside, past the zoo and the open market to the
checkpoint where five to seven thousand men pass every morning
and evening after standing in (cattle) chutes and going through a
humiliating security check. We watch them streaming out at the
end of the day and confirm that many started their days here at
three a.m.

Our final stop is at the gracious home of Munira and Hani
Amer in the town of Mas'ha. They moved into their home when
they married thirty-one years ago. The original Israeli plan was
to bulldoze their home and farmlands to make way for a Jewish
settlement that now looms beside their property and up the hill.
They refused to leave and, after a prolonged struggle that included
international support and media, the Israeli authorities built a
concrete wall and military road adjacent to their land and surrounded the other three sides of their remaining property with

metal fencing and gates. (How do you wrap your brain around this kind of cruelty and racism?) The first time I visited them they had to request a soldier unlock the gate in order to leave their home, but they now have their own key to a smaller gate. Munira greets us smiling, wearing a long black robe and hijab. She has a dimple on her chin and laughing eyes and frequently covers her face with her hands when she finds something funny. I do not know why she is not psychotic.

Over mint tea, we recount the bizarre saga and admire the lush fruit and vegetable garden she has recently planted. Plump pomegranates hang over our heads and the tomatoes, corn, and olive trees in the raised bed that is now her front lawn (the Israeli forces removed the top soil, which she has replaced) are looking pretty delicious. Gorgeous purple and pink flowers hug one of the house's stucco walls. A military jeep stops, unlocks a gate, and speeds through. The settlers from El Kana frequently harass her, throw rocks, enter her property, or attack the crops growing on other family land where her husband is now working. They have raised four sons and two daughters, have four grandchildren, and she is in remarkably good humor. She makes some of the best *za'atar* I have tasted. She has planted red and yellow flowerbeds around the outside of the house. A sweet, cooling breeze blows across the patio, and small grey birds flit in the bushes. The sky is pale blue and glows where it reaches the land. Munira talks about drawing her strength from her land; her hands have the brown thickness of a woman who knows the earth.

I kiss both her cheeks and thank her for the honor of visiting. I try to grapple with this utterly insane situation: A garden of Eden blooming in the depths of hell.

This is the gate at a terminal built for day laborers leaving Qalqilya to work in Israel, usually in industry, construction, or the black market, without any labor protections or guaranteed income. Five to seven thousand men line up at three a.m. every morning in metal chutes to pass through the humiliating checkpoint and return for a similar process in the afternoon.

The iconic concrete, eight-meter-high separation wall in Qalqilya, with security cameras and guard towers, changed the drainage and created areas of open sewerage, which floods during the rain, and confiscated massive amounts of agricultural land, undermining the local economy and creating an enormous urban prison.

June 16, 2014

The Main Course

The Balata Refugee Camp in Nablus is a concrete maze of twisting, narrow, sometimes shoulder-width paths, two main streets for the schools and the markets, and a jumble of houses leaning towards each other at odd angles, obliterating the sunshine as the residents search for nonexistent space for growing families and multiple generations. The camp started in 1950 with a lease from the town of Balata for one square kilometer of land for five thousand refugees mostly from Yaffa from the 1948 war, which explains the name of the guest house (Yaffa Guest House) where we are staying. The United Nations set up tents that turned into tiny, cramped, one-room houses and finally this jumble of construction. Sewer and water arrived in the 1960s. The houses are dark, small (mostly nine to twelve square meters per family, which is typically large and multigenerational), fairly stark, wires dangle between buildings and the rare geranium. Bright graffiti adorns some walls and Japanese artists have painted a kaleidoscope of flowers near the girl's school, which has 2,100 students, and the boy's school of 1,000 (if they actually graduate). After ninth grade the students study outside the camp.

So, let's stop a minute. Ten years without sewer or water? There is no privacy between or within houses, there is no more room to build (forget green space and play grounds), there is massive unemployment (estimated at 56% in a population of thirty thousand) and little hope or opportunity. It is hard to escape this environment, so people live their lives, marry their sweethearts, have families, take care of each other, and struggle from day to day. If you have the misfortune to suffer from a heart attack or ruptured appendix or a bleeding pregnancy, you have to be carried (I am not talking on a gurney here) down these twisted concrete paths, often turning sharply angled corners, the stone surfaces irregular and rocky, to get to an ambulance. If you are dead, the corpse sometimes is hoisted roof to roof across houses to get to a wider street. If you are in a wheelchair, if you are trying to bring in newly bought furniture, if you are having a seizure or a stroke, the hurdles are unimaginable.

Remember this the next time someone discussing the "peace process" says nonchalantly, "Oh the refugees are off the table." The refugees are actually the main course. You can imagine why Balata was one of the leaders in the two intifadas; even the dead are angry.

We sit around a long oblong table, and Mahmoud breaks into an engaging warm smile. He is a successful son of Balata. Born in the camps, he received an excellent education from UNRWA schools, and as the oldest child, went on to higher education at Birzeit University and studied and worked all over the world including the United States; his siblings are high level professionals. He presents us with a very worrisome report that mirrors our discussion the last time he spoke to our delegation: years of Palestinian dehumanization and resistance and Israeli retaliation; thousands injured, dead, imprisoned; generations of children traumatized by violence and the frequent experience of Israeli soldiers, tanks, artillery, and Apache helicopters.

As I write this blog, my thoughts are interrupted by repeated bouts of rapid gunfire. I am starting to fear this is not a wedding celebration. After all, Hebron in the south is under curfew after three Jewish yeshiva students were kidnapped (no one mentioned the six Palestinian boys disappeared from their beds in the tiny town of Asira last week, but I digress), and people are a little edgy. Netanyahu is ramping up the rhetoric and arresting Palestinians; one was reportedly killed.

Mahmoud is not optimistic. In Balata, "life is a war." The children who were out of school for months during curfews during the Second Intifada are the teenagers who are now illiterate, violent, and difficult to engage. Mahmoud runs programs for youth: music, arts, crafts, computers, film, photography, psychosocial support. He sees the depression, the rising drug abuse, and the suicidality (boys walk unarmed into Jewish settlements hoping to be killed and martyred). He notes that especially with boys aged ten to fifteen, 50% of ninth graders are illiterate and cannot even write their names. The girls do better; they are more protected, have less exposure to the street, and in general are more focused, resilient, and studious. And then those folks who actually get employed barely make a minimum wage; most people in Balata are becoming vegetarians. One kilogram of meat costs fifty shekels; many men work all day for forty. So who is going to buy meat? Mahmoud worries about the future. "Look around at the radicalism taking over the world, even in Denmark where 27% voted for an extreme right candidate. Craziness brings craziness, fanaticism brings more fanaticism."

He admits that his well-educated brother does not know how to deal with his own son. This is a very angry generation that does not see a future for itself. Even Mahmoud's seven-year-old son, who lives in a nice apartment with trees and a park outside the camp, said to his father, "'I want you to get us out of this country. This is not a country, there is no happiness here. Everybody is sad, nobody laughs.' Of course, he is right." He thinks of the struggles his parents endured, his father working as a bank employee barely able to feed his six children, all of the energy and effort that went into educating the next generation, the immense suffering and trauma his mother experienced. Born in 1948 from parents who fled the area near the future Ben Gurion airport, she was born in a cave, had seven children herself, cradled them when they were shot, injured, imprisoned, and she herself was beaten during the Second Intifada while trying to stop the IDF soldiers from invading her house. Mahmoud says softly in a broken heartfelt voice, "She has never had justice."

The future? He is more optimistic about women, their strength, focus and perseverance. He urges us to educate our communities in the US, to vote and pressure our governments. "We do not hate Jewish people, we want justice and peace for everyone…the voices of reason all losing the ground."

The rounds of gunfire are now accompanied by throbbing boisterous music. I am voting bachelor party.

Later in the day we tour the Old City of Nablus, which dates back some 4,500 years (the Romans and Ottomans were clearly here, but they were latecomers) and is surrounded by mountains splattered with houses, mosques, and twinkling lights. Much like Jerusalem, there is a maze of stone streets, halls, walkways, arched roofs, endless markets selling trinkets, fruits and vegetables, electronics, schlock Chinese products, Palestinian pastries, dresses, hijabs, and an occasional gem. There are rows of mannequin heads, each wrapped in a more creative and alluring scarf; I guess you make your fashion statement where you can. There is a musty smell of dank stones, scrawny cats, human sweat, and the occasional miraculous spice shop where we lose ourselves in the sacks of aromas and flavors while sipping bitter coffee and sniffing soap flavored with cinnamon and pomegranate. Young boys wheel carts stacked mountain high with fresh pita and we stop to fill ourselves with crispy, cheesy *kenafe* soaked in rose water. This is my kind of shopping. Most everyone is polite and solicitous and begins and ends the conversation with, "You're welcome." Little boys ask where we are from and how old we are. I keep spotting splatters of old bullet holes from previous battles engraved into the ancient walls and metal doors.

At one point we stop to visit the restoration project of Khan Al Wakala, a former market place dating back to the Romans, now owned by the Nablus Municipality. In the 2002 Israeli invasion, part of this extensive building was bulldozed by Israeli tanks to create an opening for tanks to enter the old city. (The tanks weren't made for the winding stone paths.) They destroyed numerous other ancient buildings to make openings for their machinery of war. The renovation is spectacular, with rows of columns and a lovely open floor space (formerly for animals), rooms for businesses, meetings, a restaurant, a hotel, and incredible rooftop vistas. We take in the hills of Nablus, spot the Israeli security tower that apparently has an unobstructed view of all of us in the city (that's me with the floppy hat and water bottle taking your picture) as well as all the way to Iraq. On another hilltop there is a massive orange-pink palace that is owned by the gazzillionare brother of the guy who is funding the city of Rawabi. The view is breathtaking and there is a brave little kite flying serenely above all of this chaos and insanity.

The only hitch is that the Municipality has not found an investor to finance and develop this very good idea. Any millionaires out there interested in socially responsible investing? I highly recommend this as an investment opportunity, the craftsmanship is excellent, there is an up-to-date institutional sized kitchen with shiny modern equipment, lovely stone tiles in the bathrooms; you can even see the original Roman tiles and the old well…oh, but of course, this is Nablus.

We drag ourselves back to the Yaffa Guest House, a few bites of *kenafe* has a way of slowing us down, and we are met by a pack of ten-year-olds pointing plastic guns at us, making shooting sounds, and demanding our money. But this is Balata where real children have guns and real people die and this was a little too real for me.

June 17, 2014

Walking with Ghosts

The gunfire stops around midnight and we sleep well at the Yaffa Cultural Center in the Balata Refugee Camp. In the morning we learn that the Israeli military made an early incursion into the camp, arresting about ten young men, beating one and trashing a house. This is apparently so normal that children are smiling, holding hands, and walking to school in their blue and white uniforms, men are opening their shops, and women hurry by. There is an air of total normalcy in a totally abnormal place.

We cruise through a variety of checkpoints including the once onerous Huwarra checkpoint, which is totally deserted. I watch the signs: Pisgat Zeev, Newe Yalakov, Moshe Dyan Street, the east and west-ness of Jerusalem is no longer about location but rather about where exactly Arabs and Jews are currently living. We meet up with Umar Ighbariyah from the Israeli organization Zochrot (Remembering) for a poignant, powerful tour of Lifta. The sign at the top of the valley says En Leftoah (a Biblical reference to a place that may or may not have existed here) with Lifta in parentheses. Lifta is an example of the estimated 650 depopulated Palestinian villages from 1948, but every town has its own particular tragic history. Many are unaware that the depopulations continued into the early 1950s (after the war was over) and included Zacharia and al-Majdal Asqalan. Roman tax documents document the existence of Lifta from the twelfth century, it was liberated from the Turks by Saladin in 1189, and later occupied by the Ottomans, the British, and then . . .

In the British partition plan in 1947, Lifta was supposed to be part of the international zone consisting of Jerusalem and Bethlehem, but the Zionist forces wanted an open passage between Jaffa and Jerusalem and Lifta was in the way. Lifta is much greater than the classic photos of stone houses clinging to the hillside; it actually extends up near Jaffa Street, the walls of the Old City, Mount Scopus, and includes land that now houses the Knesset, the Prime Minister's House, the High Court, and part of Hebrew University. Hana, one of our tour leaders, notes that her family still has the deed for that land. This is no longer a theoretical historical discussion.

In January 1948 (before the beginning of the war), members of the Irgun attacked a Lifta café, killing six and injuring seven. Frightened families retreated into the center of the village. This was a large, wealthy town of three thousand people with extensive agriculture, gardens, pools, and irrigation. The following month there were more attacks by the Irgun and Haganah, and gradually the families fled in terror mostly to East Jerusalem and Ramallah. After 1948, subsequent inhabitants included Jews from Arab countries placed on the "periphery" (after all, the Ashkenazim would not live here!), Jewish squatters, drug users, even a Jewish terror cell that planned to explode the Al Aqsa Mosque and did successfully bomb a bus to Hebron.

We stand at the top of the valley avoiding rumbling trucks at a massive construction site that is destined to be a fast train from Tel Aviv to Jerusalem; there are two tunnels in the distant hills that will soon connect; interestingly the tracks are supposed to go through Imwas, which is our next destination. Below this site is the continued "secret" construction of the bunker designed for government officials in the case of a nuclear holocaust. There is something supremely ironic about this location for that. (Will the whole country someday be a disappeared village?) Turning slowly 360 degrees, Umar points out the locations of other former villages, such as Colunia, Deir Yassin, and Ein Karem as well as the Jewish settlement of Romama and the Palestinian neighborhoods of Beit Hanina in East Jerusalem and Biddu in the West Bank. Umar explains that the Jewish settlement of Ramot, which is on the way to Ramallah, is actually located in the ever expanding Jerusalem, 90% built on Palestinian land. This area of patchwork claims and identities is strategically located and in 1948 was perched on the dangerous armistice border with Jordan. The border is now marked with a line of Jewish National Fund forests. Ben Gurion is reported to have said with satisfaction, "The area… is clean of strangers [Arabs]."

We start the hike down the dusty rocky valley, gracious stone ruins with magnificent arches, domes, and towering saber cactus still stand as living testaments to the past. I can almost feel the women with their bread, the men returning from the olive orchards, the children washing in the pools, the ghosts of Lifta breathing life into painful memories. Fig trees, expansive oaks, and fruit trees bear witness as well. We meet an older, mustached man, beaming with happiness. He is from here, but now lives in San Diego and is exploring the park with his nephew, who has just been released from thirteen years in prison after being arrested for involvement with the Popular Front for the Liberation of Palestine. We watch him bear hug an olive tree and start singing and dancing. He tells us he wishes he lived here so he could invite us to his home for dinner and reminds Hana in Arabic not to say anything bad about Jews! His joy is infectious and his nephew appears quietly pleased and supportive. We learn that the nephew was in a prison near Gaza; recently he was awakened in the night, put into a jeep, and dropped off in the Negev. He was found by Bedouins and gradually made his way home. He had never seen a cell phone. His mother and father were both arrested when he was released so that they would have difficulty searching for him. Does this sound strangely barbaric to anyone in the modern democratic State of Israel?

Young ultra-orthodox boys run down the path to the pools which date back to the Romans for a refreshing dip and splash. I summon up my tolerance but all I can imagine is that (even in their brightly colored underwear and wet *payus*, the *tzizit*, *tallit*, black hats, and dark suits hanging from trees) they are from some other planet; perhaps a lost lunar landing that does not see or appreciate the history and treasured beauty of this sacred space. Or is that sensibility entirely lost when a person believes so deeply in Zionism and the path Israel has taken? Do we even have a common language? Do we even see the same people?

The city plans to throw out the remaining squatters and drug users living in the ruins, and build a large complex of luxury hotels and malls. I am sure the ads may be appearing in the *New York Times* in the near future, but the plans are frozen in the courts. White butterflies flit by as if to say, you are planning what?

Umar's family history dates back to a village near Nazareth; attacked in 1948, villagers fled to the forests for two years, a few houses were destroyed and vandalized, the cows were stolen, the sugar and oil trashed, one donkey was killed (soldiers will be soldiers after all). The families were then allowed to return but in one of those ironic moments, at the Rhodes agreement with Jordan, the Israelis wanted more land near their armistice line, so the King of Jordan dipped his thumb in ink, pressed it onto the map, and poof, Umar's village was included in the State of Israel. Forty-five thousand Palestinians were annexed in this fashion and then had the privilege of Israeli citizenship and military rule until 1966. The French representative reportedly took his green pen and drew the armistice line, and hence the Green Line. Colonial powers can be so artistic and thoughtful!

Working with Zochrot, Umar notes that the media and the public have a much greater awareness of the Palestinian Nakba, although many feel that it was justified, war is hell, etc., etc. I suspect that the ghosts feel otherwise. They watch every Nakba Day, when inhabitants from Lifta now living in East Jerusalem are allowed to clean up the cemetery, honor their dead, and try to save some remnants of this magnificent city gone to ruin.

Umar Ighbariyah, from the Israeli organization Zochrot (Remembering), takes us on a powerful and poignant tour of the Palestinian village of Lifta, one of the 650 Palestinian villages depopulated in 1948.

Dating back to the twelfth century, Lifta is now a collection of houses, mosques, other buildings, and gardens lying in ruins. The population fled after multiple attacks by the Irgun and Haganah, starting in January 1948. Hana, one of our tour leaders, notes that her family still has the deed for their land here.

The Stones Do Not Lie

After a frightening moment with a billowing forest fire, we meet Umar in the village of Imwas in the middle of Canada-Ayalon Park, a major Jewish National Fund (JNF) nature reserve, popular for picnics and strolls in the woods amongst the "Roman ruins." Arabs here date back to 638 AD, when they arrived along with the bubonic plague. Archeologists think the bathhouse dates back to the third century. The village was built hundreds of years ago and, along with Yallo and Deir Ayyoub, comprised a strategically important area called the Latrun. Israel forces tried and failed to seize the Latrun in 1948 because the local Arabs put up fierce opposition, and thus the Israelis lost a direct route from Jaffa to Jerusalem. The generals called their alternative route The Burma Road, evoking a fought over supply route between Burma and China, scene of a number of important struggles during World War II. By referencing the language of the Allies who fought the Germans, the framing about the struggle to supply Jerusalem easily shifted: the Arabs became the new Nazis. The capture of Latrun was one of the first goals of the 1967 War. Much to my amazement (and I am pretty hard to amaze at this point), the village was occupied in 1967 but never annexed like East Jerusalem, so the area is technically still in the West Bank as occupied territory. Nonetheless, Israelis frolic freely in the park, and inhabitants of the three old villages have to obtain permits to visit the sites of their former homes, schools, olive groves, desecrated cemeteries, etc. In 1967, the villagers, by the way, gave no resistance; the Israeli Defense Forces rounded them up in the central yard, reassured them they would return soon, and then forcibly marched the bewildered families toward Ramallah. "Yalla to Ramallah." A few hid in their homes, a few fled to a Trappist monastery, but a total of seventy-five hundred villagers were ethnically cleansed. Umar shows us photos that look eerily like 1948, and dare I say, other catastrophes that have befallen people we all know and love.

Once the inhabitants were gone, the army bulldozed the houses, but the stones and protruding pipes and metal remain, as well as a sixth century Byzantine church, a crumbling Roman bathhouse, and three neglected cemeteries. After the Six Day War, the inhabitants

June 18, 2014

The World According to Sami

Last night, as we leave Elbeit Alnisa'i for dinner, the nine of us wander off into the dark streets of Beit Sahour, past churches and statues of the Virgin Mary, tempting pastry shops, and a clear starry sky, challenged by sidewalks begging for unsteady ankles. A small elderly woman with a twinkle in her eye who hosts us at the hostel with a steady stream of mint tea and Turkish coffee, takes H. by the elbow and leads us determinedly up and down the hills and winding streets to a lovely restaurant complete with sappy music and the World Cup on a large screen. Later, overstuffed once again by tasty rice, cauliflower, eggplant, watermelon, and more, we set off on our uncertain course home and immediately find ourselves in the midst of ten or so teenage boys on bikes doing various testosterone-driven things that boys do. In any other city I would feel afraid, but we soon find ourselves surrounded by these young men who carefully herd us back to our guest house, leaving us with the customary, "You're welcome!"

Tonight I am writing from the bosom of a family living in a refugee camp in Bethlehem and once again the extraordinary decency and generosity is overwhelming. The house is multistory with various adjoining apartments, kitchens, bathrooms, a large room filled with rubble which is under construction, and a spiral staircase in the kitchen that seems to lead to another apartment where the four girls sleep. There is definitely a baseline level of calm, organized chaos. The parents have two more sons: one who is busy studying for final exams, the other who is severely disabled with cerebral palsy, partly related to a premature birth and then another episode of severe oxygen loss while hospitalized, maybe from infection. Mostly he sits curled in a swing in the hall that seems made from a seat in a car, and rocks back and forth, making various cries and calling "Ma." His mother tenderly explains that she understands him, as do his siblings. At night, he sleeps curled up with her. He attended a special school for a while, but the family wanted him home because the teacher did not understand him and he cried all the time. He is also fourteen years old and tall for his age, increasingly difficult to carry, and facing an educational system with inadequate resources or understanding for children with multiple severe problems. There are fifty children now at home in the three Bethlehem refugee camps with disabilities and enormous needs, mostly met by their unbelievably supportive families.

I meet the paternal grandmother who, like me, was born in 1948 but, unlike me, looks like a fragile eighty-year-old who has lived through an inordinately large amount of stress. She smiles, enjoys holding hands, and prays quietly with her beads. She asks me why I am travelling without my husband and lets me know that if I were her daughter, I would be killed. I give her a quick rendition of a modern American marriage and assure her that my husband and I love and respect each other very much. Everyone seems impressed that I am a doctor. This seems to put the issue to rest.

Various nieces and nephews drift in and out, and I think the family is also caring for the son and daughter of the father's brother, who was killed ten years ago. Pictures of the martyred uncle adorn the living room, where we drink tea and then chop a mountain of tomatoes, baked eggplant, and onion. Caution: large wonderful meal ahead. The puzzles, finger puppets, origami, and magic markers emerge from our bags, and suddenly the children are very preoccupied. There is a lot of touching and cooperation, laughter, playful shoving and hugging, and a sweetness to the interactions. At dinner, the disabled son is carried into the dining room and is hugged, kissed, and fed by a variety of family members (much like a baby bird with a broken wing in a nest with foragers bringing back delicacies). They all clearly love and accept him and are not at all distracted by his movements and behavior. Somehow, this kind of full acceptance and support makes me want to cry.

I have been trying to keep track of the events that are heating up all around us. Three Israeli settler boys from Hebron (read right-wing, ultra-Orthodox) were apparently kidnapped, and while this is to be utterly condemned in general, their disappearance is being used to whip the country into a wild, xenophobic, Hamas-hating, unity government-hating mood. Everywhere we see large signs on buses, "Bring our boys home!" and there are special hashtags and quite a media frenzy. Prime Minister Netanyahu seems convinced this is the work of Hamas despite what seems to be a lack of carefully collected evidence, the Israeli Defense Forces are making massive arrests, people have been injured and shot by the soldiers, a friend of mine was hit by a tear gas canister while protesting the force-feeding of the hunger strikers in Israeli jails, and we keep hearing that the city of Hebron is under closure, with a massive military presence throughout the West Bank.

While I understand the terror and horror of kidnapping teenage boys, Palestinian children and teenagers have been detained and arrested (isn't it kidnapping if it is done by an arm of the state acting in an utterly egregious manner????) often in the middle of the night in front of terrified mothers and fathers, with no lawyers, and often no charges. Big surprise, there has been no public outrage for these Arab children and obviously no collective punishment of Israeli families whose sons have been beating and cuffing and interrogating frightened kids, ignoring international law and common decency. It all feels different when the victim and perpetrator are flipped, doesn't it?

So we are back in what is often called '48 Israel, i.e., the Israel contained within the increasingly phantasmagorical Green Line, and we are meeting with one of my favorite academic-activists, former city councilor Sami Abu Shehadeh. The focus is Yaffa and the subtitle is mixed cities and racism. Sami notes that the poet Mahmoud Darwish once said that most wars end with, "we are here and they are there," but in this war, no such separation occurred. More than 90% of the historical Palestinian population lives in total separation from the Jewish population, but the boundaries are very messy. Until recently, he explains, with his ironic mix of deprecating humor and truth telling, there was no need to legalize the process of separation, but in the past decade, Arabs (Israelis deny that there are Palestinians in Israel, so they are called Arabs), have tried to move into Jewish areas (better housing, better schools, better services), and because there were no racial laws in Israel, a new criteria was invented. People can be excluded from communities because of "unsuitable compatibility." Who are we fooling here? At Tel Aviv University, a professor noted that Tel Aviv is the only Western city without an Arab community and also the Western city with the closest Arab adjoining community in the world, i.e. Jaffa.

As we wander the streets of Jaffa, through shabby neighborhoods and gentrified streets and glorious views of the Mediterranean and elegant, expensive old Arab houses now developed or bought for foreign embassies, wealthy Jews, etc., Sami explains there are two main narratives around a particular point in the run up to the 1948 war and they are in total disagreement, as is much of the discourse in Israel. The Zionist narrative states that in January 1948, two months after partition but before the war, this central market area where we are standing had buildings housing Arab terrorists, threatening Tel Aviv, and two heroic Stern Gang soldiers brought a truck loaded with explosives into the central market and blew the place up. A major Zionist victory.

The Palestinian narrative states that while there was a lot of violence resisting British occupation and Zionist expansion, there was no Palestinian army, and Arab armies could not reach Jaffa. The Saray House in the market place was used by ordinary people and in fact held an orphanage which was blown up by Zionist terrorists, murdering innocent children. A major Zionist massacre. Framing is everything.

As we find refuge in the shade, Sami reflects on the historical importance of Jaffa, which was even mentioned in the Old Testament when King Solomon brought cedar from Lebanon through Jaffa to build the temple, and then the prophet Jonah had that unfortunate incident with the whale and got spit up on some lonely Jaffa Beach. Not that any of this matters for the present, right?

He notes that there are two types of Palestinian historians: those who believe Palestinians are Europeans who immigrated from Crete and settled in the Levant, and those who are pan-Arabic. Palestinians arrived from the Arab peninsula and, oh by the way, that was around 12,000 years ago. Everyone else then arrived to occupy this spot, the perfect seaport, the center of commerce, the gateway to Palestine. Jaffa was occupied some 30 times and obviously had its times of success and times of neglect. But Palestinians were clearly here first: not that any of this matters for the present, right?

The big deal happened in modern history with the famous Jaffa orange export business. Apparently some stroke of genius or luck led to the production of a thick-skinned orange that could be shipped anywhere, the Shamuti orange, carefully wrapped in special paper. So an enormous industry was created: the growers, the pickers, the wrappers, the guys who built the special boxes, the transport to the port, the boats, you get the picture. In the 1930s, five million boxes of oranges, containing 400 million oranges, passed through the port of Jaffa. (So much for the Arabs' inability to make the desert bloom, and their backward agricultural processes!) Tel Aviv was founded in the late 19th century as a neighborhood of Jaffa with some 100 Jewish families. As Sami notes, "Before 1948, people came to work in Jaffa from all over the Arab world and now we Palestinians leave to work all over the Arab world." The ebb and flow of history, and it is clearly not done with the ebbing and flowing part.

This all ended with the 1948 war, when Jaffa was largely depopulated of its Arab population. After the war, Israelis passed an aggressive program of Judaization, changing Arabic signage, destroying the Old City, and disappearing the history and culture of the Palestinian majority that had existed for centuries (I think this part is important for today, right?). With British support, Tel Aviv became a city in 1909; by 1919 there were two thousand Jewish inhabitants, and by 1948 the number had reached two hundred thousand.

In the unforgiving sun, we admire the famous Clock Tower, built in 1901 by the Ottomans; across the street was the Ottoman prison which became the British and then the Israeli police station. (Must be a trend?) It is slated to become a fancy boutique hotel with its northern wall adjacent to the mosque of Jaffa. The history of this city is embedded in its architecture, and sometimes I feel the walls are weeping when they are not outright screaming for our attention. We wander through the old covered market, now mostly cheap Chinese imports, a herd of Birthright kids, signs for a Lady Gaga concert, and tattooed bikers and rainbow hair. We are standing in front of three hundred new apartments, this is gentrification on steroids, upscale bars and cafes now appear like mushrooms after a spring rain. Sami teases, there are now hairdressers for dogs, and in Tel Aviv more couples have dogs and cats than children. Welcome to the twenty-first century, when pet adoption and doggy daycare are the norm, but no one has the money or motivation to support a severely disabled Palestinian boy.

We wander by the Scottish Church, the Old French Hospital, Saint Joseph's School for Boys (soon to be a boutique hotel)—the colonists and religious institutions were busy for a long time; there are a long list of stories about Jesus and his disciples, miracles, visions, angels, etc. that relate to Jaffa. The impact of that is now mostly apparent in a very strong tourism industry, focused on visiting all the cities in the New Testament. Religion in the service of capitalism.

Sami notes sarcastically, "Then there was the most important real estate invention: The View." We pass by the upscale Andromeda Hills project, the most expensive housing project in Jaffa, gated illegally, tied up in court battles, and now for the past ten years gated "for the public safety." Really? He notes ironically, in the past at the sea, poor people used to smoke hashish, and now at the sea, rich people smoke hashish. Rents are as high as twenty thousand dollars per month and houses sell for millions.

We look up at a large poster of Handala done by the cartoonist and political activist, Naji Al Ali. In the poster, an American in Lebanon is asking for the religious identity of an Arab (I think there are sixteen types of religious identities in Lebanon), and the guy replies, "I am an Arab and you are a donkey." Subtle? The Handala character stands nearby with his back to us and spikey cactus hair. Naji, a Palestinian living in Lebanon, left for his own personal safety to Kuwait and then to London, where he was assassinated in 1987. There are so many theories about who pulled the trigger. He pretty much offended everyone by speaking the truth to power. Sami explains that Handala came to Naji in a dream, a small child who would help him tell the truth. Naji said he left Palestine when he was ten and Handala will only grow up when Naji returns. He turns his back to the viewer because the world has turned its back on Palestine. His hair is spikey because reality is bitter. He is now the most famous Arab symbol of perseverance and resistance in the world.

This brings us back to the Palestinians of 1948 and the neighborhood of Ajami (see the film of the same name and my blog posts from previous delegations). In 1948, the remaining Palestinian inhabitants were rounded up and put into the neighborhood of Ajami; their houses were declared neglected, and they were declared present absentees, or they kept their houses and had to share with incoming Jewish immigrants. Sami's great-grandfather was a soldier in the Ottoman Army; he was not willing be a refugee so he stayed, was sent to Ajami, and lived surrounded by fences, soldiers, and dogs. Even the European Jews called it the ghetto. They should know.

These refugees (thirty-nine hundred left out of a population of one hundred twenty thousand) experienced the dispossession of the Nakba and the loss of all friends, family possessions, libraries, teachers, doctors, hospitals, and language ("the biggest armed robbery in the twentieth century"). They experienced the fact that if the Israelis wanted cheap labor, Palestinians were present, but if Palestinians wanted their homes back, they were absent. This was a humiliating personal and economic loss that led to decades of depression, drug abuse, alcoholism, and criminality. In 1950, Jaffa was annexed to Tel Aviv and since then it has been run *by* Jews and planned *for* Jews "in this liberal democracy of Israel." Until 1993, Palestinians were not even statistically counted as a separate group. Haneen Zoabi, the Palestinian Knesset member who recently criticized the hyper response to the kidnappings of the yeshiva students, is now facing death threats and being called a traitor.

So how does this segregation and racism look up close and personal? In the mixed cities, there are three kinds of schools: secular Jewish, religious Jewish, and Arab. Some 20 to 25% of Arabs go to secular Jewish schools where the education is better, though completely Zionist. Jewish parents complained when the Arabs reached 50% of the student body, so the school divided itself into two schools, Arab and Jew. Then the parents demanded a wall down the middle of the playground. The municipality refused and used words like multiculturalism, so the Jewish parents took their kids out and sent them to schools in Tel Aviv, or to the right-wing national religious schools. The Israelis do not even seem to have the inclination or institutional or legal building blocks to build a multicultural society, let alone face the glaring endemic racism.

It is late and I am too tired to continue. Let me just say that I knew I was in '48 Israel when I ordered a Turkish coffee and a lovely cappuccino arrived. I didn't want to complain, so I grabbed the cinnamon, sprinkled the steamed foam liberally, only to discover that it was actually pepper.

Scarlet Johansson Has Gas

Spending a few hours with Tamer Nafar, the hip-hop artist for the group DAM (see the incredible documentary "Slingshot Hip Hop") is always a trip. The drive to Lyd (on Israeli maps: Lod) where he lives involves passing Ben Gurion Airport, built on the lands of Lydda, speaking of dispossession. Lyd is a "mixed city" with an ancient bloody and complicated history without any of the touchy feely reconciliation stuff that "mixed" may imply today. I always think it should be called a "mixed up city." The place consists of Palestinians (excuse me, we are in Israel so they are officially Arabs) and a mix of Jewish Ethiopians, Moroccans, and other Jews from lower socioeconomic groups. We are on a bus touring the area and Tamer never seems to age; he reminds me of a tiger about to pounce; he speaks his mind freely, crackles with sarcasm and energy, and has no verbal sensors (in keeping I suppose with being a well-known hip-hop artist!), though he seems a bit tamer now that he has a wife and son. Parenthood will do that.

We see more blaring signs on buses: "Bring back our boys!" The political frenzy is heating up and I fear what is coming. We start in a dusty, run-down center near the Great Mosque where Palestinians were first rounded up in 1948 and massacred by the Stern Gang. One hundred and thirty people died and one survived buried under the corpses. The mosque was closed until 1994. Tamer remarks that an Israeli reporter noted that the walls of the reopened mosque were washed, but the blood soaked floor was just covered with carpets. And to think I grew up believing that Jewish soldiers only fought noble and moral wars; we did not massacre, we protected women, children, and fruit trees, we learned from our history... the making and unmaking of founding mythology is powerful, challenging work.

Tamer reviewed much of the city's history and the various neighborhoods and their related ethnicities and socioeconomics (no surprise, the whiter the Jews, the more services, sidewalks, clean streets; the more Arab, the less of everything). If we look at today, he sees the main Zionist dilemma is one of demography. The cry now is to build a new, "clean" city, "Yehud Lud," bring in the extremist Jewish settlers (some from Gaza, some from France) and place them in the middle of Palestinian neighbors. Palestinians facing poverty, hostile Hassids, and little hope are faced with selling their properties to these settlers or to the drug dealers that dominate many of the neighborhoods. These are not good choices. And thus the Palestinian presence is steadily disappeared. Part of a Jewish apartment complex is located on a Muslim cemetery, so Tamer can no longer visit his father's grave. According to Tamer, approximately 90% of the funding in Lyd is budgeted to build housing for Jews. He notes ironically that of $12 million, $2 million is for Jewish schools and services, $2 million for Jewish neighborhoods, $6 million for a separation wall (!) in the city, and $2 million to demolish Arab houses. Trends?

The neglected, poorer parts of the city are infested with drug dealers (he points out one with an "ATM," i.e., a hole in the wall where you put your shekels and get your drugs—I did not try it even in the interests of journalism), and the only rehab center used to be owned by a drug dealer whose son committed suicide and then the father changed his tune. Mostly folks are using crystal meth, coke, and pills; the dealers are often Arabs and Bedouin clans. As Tamer says, "Not a tasty salad."

The confounding disaster is of course racism. Tamer explains that intellectually he feels sympathy for Ethiopian Jews, who are also on the bottom of the socioeconomic ladder; but then he "has to be fucked over by an Ethiopian (Jewish) policeman who is trying to be soooo Israeli." Recently there was a scandal when it was found that hospitals were throwing out blood donations from Ethiopian donors and that Ethiopian women were being sterilized without consent. Racial purity anyone?

With his family and a successful music career, Tamer has moved to a nicer neighborhood; his son is attending an Arabic-language preschool and speaks it fluently. The parents are now teaching him Hebrew at home; after all, he does need to speak the language of the colonizer. Tamer fears that if he went to a Jewish preschool, he would lose his Arab identity. These are tough issues to negotiate.

We meander towards the "wrong side of the tracks," where there is a railroad station, originally built by the British for Palestinian workers. Now the neighborhood is only visited by junkies, police, and settlers, "They have the country, we have the streets." This impoverished shantytown is limited by a nearby *moshav* (a Jewish community), the train tracks, a highway, and a Jewish neighborhood. While there are successful doctors and lawyers here, there is mostly a lot of poverty and unemployment. These folks are not accepted in Jewish neighborhoods. One hundred and fifty Palestinian houses (remember, all citizens of the great democracy of Israel), have been demolished due to lack of permits, but since these are unrecognized neighborhoods, there is no system to apply for anything, not that that would work anyway. And each group blames the group less fortunate: Ethiopians and Moroccans are part of the problem and they blame the Palestinians. Ironically, the millions of shekels spent on house demolitions could be used to create a viable public housing system. But this is Israel.

Tamer notes this whole insanity is actually about Judaizing Lyd. He quips that the Jews are always complaining that the Palestinians want to throw them into the sea, but in actuality it was the Jewish forces that pushed the Palestinian civilians into the Mediterranean. Tamer's grandfather was "thrown into a boat" in 1948 and there are plenty of historical photos that document that frantic expulsion.

But there is a bureaucracy to racism and Judaization. Palestinian land was declared "frozen" and cannot be developed. Ten years ago, Jewish Russian neighborhoods were built on frozen land with full infrastructure and no permits. They received their retroactive permits two years ago.

And then there are the railroad tracks, all eight of them, 250 trains a day. We hold our breaths and watch kids scamper across the tracks as the lights flash and the rails come down. Well before 2006, there were no lights and no guardrails, some fifteen children were killed. Tamer made a video with the late Juliano Mer Khamis (actor and founder of the Jenin Freedom Theater) and took Israeli rock stars to this neighborhood with the media in tow, creating intense public pressure, and poof, lights and guard rails. Can you imagine such a situation in a posh neighborhood in Tel Aviv? But then they would have moved the train tracks… The promised pedestrian tunnel or bridge has yet to materialize, but no one else has been crushed by an oncoming train. I counted four trains in the few minutes we had this conversation.

We head into a dirt path, concrete walls, corrugated metal walls and roofs, piles of trash, open sewerage, bedding hung in the sun, purple bougainvillea flaunting itself. Where are we? A shanty town in Brazil? South Africa? A ten-ish-year-old girl offers our bus driver a nice drug purchase. Israel, the big success story, the start-up nation, the light unto the nations? This is shameful.

One positive development Tamer explains is that at the site of a previous demolition, a new shiny school, the Ort School of Science and Engineering, has been built, his wife teaches here, the principal is an Arab. She describes herself as apolitical, but she knows how to work the system, she is well-respected, she goes out on the streets and talks to the drug dealers, and she gets excellent results. All of her students are Palestinian.

Our final stop is the Shamir neighborhood, a Palestinian area adjacent to a *moshav* that demanded a separation wall of their own to protect them from the neighboring unwelcome Arabs. Activists took them to court and they said it was "an acoustic wall" due to the trains (not), then the wall was left partially built for seven to eight years. A beautiful, multistory Palestinian apartment building was built in the neighborhood without a permit (obviously since there are no permits), and some weird deal was made not to demolish this apartment building in exchange for completing the separation wall. A very weird legal system indeed.

I ask Tamer, who is this strange mix of high energy, outrage, and cynicism, what are the main barriers for the Palestinians digging themselves out of this economic, drug-trafficking mess and he replies: "Our tribal mentality." (It seems we are all suffering from our tribal disorders, only mine has all the big guns.) But Tamer continues the good fight, pushing the boundaries, getting in everyone's face, calling things as he sees them in all their contradictions and ugliness and sarcasm. He is releasing English language hip-hop songs: "Mama, I fell in love with a Jew," and "Scarlett Johansson has gas" (a reference to the Sodastream campaign she promoted; Sodastream is produced in an illegal Israeli settlement).

He is planning a full album and is writing a script on Palestinian hip-hop. And he is using his powerful music and his sharp tongue to continue to create political change and wake up the international community through the language of hip-hop.

I leave both inspired and appalled at the consequences of the Zionist dream: of the price of privileging Jews over everyone else, white Jews over brown Jews, of the self-destruction of communities that are pushed to the edges of society, of the terrible cost of the racism that has always been part of the fabric of this contradictory place.

This is a fragment of a wooden box used to crate oranges from Jaffa; the thick-skinned Shamuti orange revolutionized the export business. In the 1930s, five million boxes of oranges containing four hundred million oranges passed through the port of Jaffa. In 1948, most of Jaffa's Palestinians fled or were actively dispossessed and Israelis took over their industries and land.

June 19, 2014

The Tigers, the Butterflies, and the Birds

Our host father and his two young daughters begin the tour of the Aida refugee camp in Bethlehem after a breakfast we prepared together with his wife. My tomato chopping skills are definitely improving. He smokes constantly and, like many men, has done his stint in Israeli jails. After two years, he was released and given a permit that limited his movements to Bethlehem for life. His family has had many Israeli home invasions, and the Israeli Defense Forces killed his brother and sister and bombed his mother's house. He has many skills in construction and is a skilled electrician; he has no paid work currently but dreams of building his wife her cooking center to raise money for their disabled son and help empower other women. IDF soldiers visited our street last night, and this morning, we can see the spirals of tear gas one hundred meters away as young boys run down the street toward the archetypal entrance to the camp (a large house key over the gate). The massive grey concrete wall at the entrance to the camp is surrounded by garbage, and a grey IDF guard tower completes the trilogy. (Think the photo of the Pope praying at this wall, saying to the world, THIS EXISTS!) It appears that the tear gas is also in the vicinity of the boys' UNRWA school and they are taking exams. Our host mentions that the IDF soldiers use the boys for target practice. The boys run towards the conflict, grabbing stones; the girls run home. The young daughter is handing out geraniums she has picked. The site of this skirmish is where the Pope stopped to kiss the wall and pray.

The camp has no green space but tons of children who need to play and release the rage, frustration, and fear that infuses the air and tear gas they breathe. We hear the history of dispossession in 1948, the UNRWA tents, the UN houses (thirty single rooms, one per family, often six to ten children and grandparents, and one bathroom for all thirty homes. Think about that for a minute; we are talking ten kids, poverty, trauma, depression, and appalling overcrowding.) Many men went to work in Israel to provide food for their families. My host explains that he is afraid for his children. He tells them to stay away from the soldiers; he deeply cares for them, the soldiers do not. "We want peace." He has Jewish Israeli friends and occasionally they visit him. He of course cannot leave Bethlehem, which is really an extension of his lifetime prison sentence. The frequent tear gassing affects everyone and is reported to increase the risk of miscarriage.

More tear gas, more boys dash by. We stop at the mosque and kindergarten. There is a painting of a fierce orange tiger and the words, "Here only tigers can survive." On the adjacent wall are two orange butterflies and the words, "Here only butterflies and birds are free." Another young boy races past. We see a church in the camp and then cautiously look at the wall a few blocks from the guard tower. There is an enormous graffiti of a boy with a slingshot. On a nearby crumbling wall of a house, someone drew an open mouth with a dove, a key in his mouth, flying out.

I spot Arabic graffiti supporting Fatah but surprisingly little related to any political party. There is a general sense of disgust for all political parties around here. I see a wall of a house with a painting of Al Aqsa and Mecca. Roosters are crowing and a haze of tear gas hangs over the homes. My host talks about wanting his children to get a good education and go to "the best universities." He, like many fathers, has great hopes. He points out the agricultural land stolen when the wall was built; land his father would have given to him as part of the next generation of sons. I see teenage boys collecting small stones, begging us for dollars, cigarettes. My host pats them on the head and mutters, "simple," and tries to dissuade them from throwing stones. They do not listen.

We make a quick friendly stop at the Al Rowwad Children's Theater to visit our friend Abdelfattah Abusrour. We have been here before (my daughter taught yoga and dance), the dabke and theater troupe have performed in the Boston area and Europe. We squeeze into Abed's office and I scan the photos of the Pope, Malcolm X, Martin Luther King, Gandhi, Mandela, Einstein, and piles of books and files. On the wall, a poster proclaims: "The Right

June 20, 2014

From Tear Gas to *Maqluba*

Feigning bravado and an ambivalent sense of group confidence, our delegation sets off for the West Bank village of Bil'in (see the documentary "Five Broken Cameras") for the weekly demonstration against the separation wall. There is no direct travel service on Fridays, so this involves several taxis and lots of negotiation. A group of Palestinians from Ramallah who hold annual conventions (usually in someplace like Detroit) for all the former inhabitants and descendants of the city are celebrating in Ramallah this year and they are unusually joyful, keeping their memories alive and grappling with today's ugly realities. One uninitiated twenty-something was shocked to learn that there are Palestinian refugees, camps, and other inconveniences his protective and perhaps traumatized parents had wished to avoid. Black flags and posters are everywhere, portraying a strong man breaking his chains over his head, in solidarity with the prison hunger strikers who are very much on everyone's minds. We hit one massive traffic jam, a combination of a checkpoint and a wedding and an army of frustrated, testosterone-driven drivers.

I think how much our delegation has really been travelling in a bubble. We have had calls from a variety of frantic family members, basically demanding, "Do you know where you are and what is happening there????" Our next-door neighbors, Syria, Iraq, and Lebanon, are imploding in various dangerous ways, the Israeli press and the Palestinian street are full of calls to avenge the missing yeshiva boys and as usual every Palestinian is a suspect. Every cab driver we talk to thinks this whole episode is a ploy to give the IDF reservists some target practice before the big post-Kerry bang. We have had almost no checkpoint delays, no anxious humiliating interrogations (expect of course for our Palestinian leader, but that is normal for her, which just shows how distorted normality is around here). We slept through the night house raids, were too far away to hear the first Israeli raid in fourteen years at Birzeit University, which involved rounding up (and emasculating) the university security guards and confiscating flags, banners, and posters from the student union, as well as searching the campus. And we live with our unconscious, mostly white American privilege, presumptions, and passports that allow us to walk the streets of cities that our Palestinian hosts can only dream of. Why we are not hated is still unclear to me, but the warmth and generosity is truly genuine.

So today we set off for some blunt reality, an unarmed resistance march against the separation wall in the town of Bil'in. Mohammed Khatib, one of the leaders of the organizing committee, wearing a tee shirt that says "Water and salt = dignity," a reference to the diet of the hunger strikers in Israeli jails, meets us at the entry to the town. He explains that Bil'in has 2,000 inhabitants, and another 2,000 living elsewhere, and 5,000 dunams of land; 3,500 dunams were confiscated by the wall and 1,500 returned after a long struggle. Soon we are sitting under a tarp on plastic chairs in his patio, sipping mint tea, and admiring his beautiful stone-polished home that he has poured years of work into creating. I see a modern kitchen, a sunken living room with a poster of a young Arafat, and an amazing fireplace carved into an ancient dead olive tree. His five-ish-year-old daughter coyly joins him, wearing a traditional embroidered dress. Our cab driver joins us too; this is, after all, a grassroots struggle.

The story of Bil'in is the common tale of land confiscation, the building of a wall starting in 2004, the massive growth of an expanding Jewish settlement, Modiin Illit (later we can see the cranes and high rises). In 2005, the Palestinian villagers started to get creative, tying themselves to their olive trees, placing themselves on the land in cages and coffins, and shocking the Israeli soldiers with their nonviolent resistance. This drew media attention but no changes on the ground. They built a caravan on the land taken by the settlements (reminiscent of the right-wing Jewish hilltop youth that often stake out claims before the official settlement is approved), which slowed the construction; the IDF said that mobile homes are illegal (except of course for Jews). So in one frenzied night, they built a fixed home with a door and windows, to the appropriate specifications, and this stopped settlement growth for one year. Ultimately the Israeli construction company actually went bankrupt. (A victory for our side!) Then the route of the wall was changed to return some of the Palestinian land and the settlement construction resumed. The Palestinians are still not allowed to work their land that they won back, though they built a (truly shocking) brightly colored playground on it (you never know what these terrorists will do), so I am not yet calling this a victory, especially since the battle is really about the end of the occupation.

Mohammed has a sense of humor born of struggle. While much of the world was focused on the World Cup in Brazil (sorry, sports fans), he helped organize a soccer match in front of the Ofer Prison, where prisoners are on a serious hunger strike. He was arrested a day before an action to block Highway 443, which cuts through the West Bank, and when the police asked him for information, he referred them to social media. (I always worry that the FBI and Shin Bet just sit in their offices reading our Facebook posts.) When they were surprised by the action, he said, "There are no secrets, but there are surprises."

Today, many will not be at this march because there was a call to pray and march at Beitunya in support of the Ofer prisoners. We set off in a row of battered cars, a motley crew of muscular looking Palestinian men with flags, press with large cameras and face masks, women of all varieties, internationals, and Israelis, and park under some olive trees. After a short discussion on safety (avoid getting bonked on the head by a tear gas canister, do not rub your eyes, do not run, cover your face with a scarf-done! Do not panic, tear gas will not kill you, it will only make you feel like you are about to die, your eyes will tear and your throat will burn, sniff an onion, an alcohol swab, anything with a smell, and DO NOT walk downwind. The IDF only use rubber bullets when stones are thrown and nobody dies from a stun grenade.) That seemed like a pretty long list to me, but we set off. We begin the march down the dusty, hot, rocky road, my brain giving me fairly strong messages about getting the hell out of there ASAP and my legs inspired by the struggle against a long list of historical injustices. My knees are sort of in between.

Before a stone can be thrown, the tear gas starts and is blown up the hill to the stragglers like me. I cannot imagine how it feels at the front of the line. Europeans remark that this tear gas seems much more powerful than they are used to and others mentioned that Israelis are always field testing new weaponry. Great! I find myself a cluster of olive trees and some other less-than-brave protestors and try to remember the rules of engagement. There are single canisters and then showers of canisters, the occasional stun grenade (very loud boom), and then rubber bullets. I am told that the Jewish settlers on the other side of the wall cheer the soldiers on and play inspiring music while they do battle with the dangerous terrorists on the other side who would like to plant their vegetables, tend their olives and otherwise lead normal lives. If the wind (and the tear gas of course) is blowing towards the settlers (one can only hope), then the IDF moves more quickly to rubber bullets. The settlers consider the blowback as some sort of badge of courage in the fight for Zionist domination. (This I confess is my own theory.) I make my way across the rocky field to where people even more frightened than me are watching, when a tear gas canister spirals through the air and lands ten feet from me. This keeps happening, reminding me again that there is actually no safe place and that the soldiers have been known to come into the town and throw tear gas into people's homes. Last week one child was shot with a rubber bullet and injured. The important thing to remember about a rubber bullet is that it is indeed a bullet. Such lovely people, these soldiers, "the most moral army in the world." Sometimes the hot canisters start small brush fires in the dry grass.

The demonstrators feel that the soldiers have been more vigorous due to all the tension around the missing boys (remember not a single stone was thrown) and the aggressive incursions and arrests that are going on all over the West Bank. Everyone talks about how these weapons are made in the United States and that the solution to the conflict lies in changing the policies of the United States. Congress, are you listening? This is really important if you can take time off from fundraising and getting ready to bomb the next people in need of democracy!

The demonstration finally winds down, although that burning feeling in the throat drags on for a while, and suddenly we find ourselves invited for lunch at another organizer's house where his wife just happens to have *maqluba* (remember that chicken and rice dish from yesterday?) and salad for some 15 people. (She must shop at the Palestinian version of Costco.) So we gather around, eat to our hearts' content, buy Palestinian embroidery from the women's cooperative, and struggle to make sense out of the insanity of occupation, land grabs, racism, hatred, entitlement, military hardware, and the power of determined resistance by ordinary people desperately trying to create political change and to build the kind of lives that we take for granted.

And for Extra Credit: Hebron

We leave for the tortured city of Hebron later than expected (tear gas, food, and embroidery), and H. (Palestinian from Ramallah, just graduated from Yale) tries to explain to me the intricacies of her permitting process. She has a West Bank ID. She can only apply for a new permit to enter Israel if her old one has already expired (it generally lasts three months). Fortunately she does not own a car or a donkey; that would also require a permit. And she cannot apply until it actually physically runs out. Are you following this? So, her permit ran out Thursday evening, the earliest she could apply is Friday, but Friday and Saturday are holidays and you cannot get any permit unless it is an emergency. If you pay 140 shekels a year for a magnetic strip card that indicates you do not have any security issues, it will take one day to get the permit, otherwise it takes two, but of course the permit is never guaranteed. So the earliest she can apply is Monday, but she needs a permit to come with us into Israel to Nazareth on Saturday, which in this crazy world is now impossible. Now let me remind you that she has just graduated from a prestigious US university, has no criminal record, has a great sense of humor, comes from a respectable family, and poses no security risks except perhaps the risk of speaking her mind, which the last time I checked was still legal in most modern democratic societies. If she decides to take her chances and sneaks in (happens a lot) and the driver gets caught, he is fined, which is really not fair to him. Under these circumstances, she would not carry any IDs, so the Israelis would not be able to punish her since they cannot prove she is who she is and you can bet I am not going to help them either on that one. So does this sound sensible? Related to security? Keeping the folks in Netanya secure in their beach chairs sipping their pomegranate mojitos? Valium anyone?

At the village of Qalandia we spot two soldiers crouching in a rotary hiding behind an olive tree, their weapons are loaded, hands on the trigger, and we are not sure if it is tear gas or bullets. I learn that a thirteen-year-old Palestinian child was killed yesterday. Ma'ale Adumim sprawls across distant hilltops like a giant snake slithering through the territories; there is an IDF jeep on the road; we come to a checkpoint with three IDF soldiers. On the radio the woman reports a loud explosion in a town near Hebron. The IDF stole fifteen thousand shekels during one home invasion and the Palestinian Authority is completely invisible except for traffic cops, who are not doing much. When the Israelis are planning a major incursion, they send their colleagues (that is too nice a word, collaborators?) home. Hebron feels eerie and tense; young men cluster on sidewalks, looking thin, hungry, and ready for trouble; large dumpsters have been placed across the roads, some already brooding smoke. Despite this, people are out on the streets, shopping, biking, driving, smoking.

I have never seen our guide, Hisham Sharabati, so tense; yes we are late, and yes he has a flat tire, but the city feels like it is about to explode, and he has a lot to teach us and wants us all to leave in one piece. (Good plan.) He reviews the outrageous history of the ancient city of Hebron and its colonization and militarization by a small number of fanatical Jews from Kiryat Arba who then decided to take over the center of the Old City and destroy the lives of the Palestinian families living there. (See my previous blogs for details.) Nonetheless, everything is worse since my last descent into this living hell: with the kidnapping of the three yeshiva students, no one with an ID who is less than fifty years old can leave the country (like the lovely man who sat next to me in the *service* and has been accepted to a USAID program on leadership development in Washington, DC, and has a formal letter from the US Consulate; he is now on his fourth try to get by the ever so conscientious Israeli security at the border with Jordan).

The Palestinian markets are not only covered with sheets and chicken wire to protect them from the garbage thrown down on them by Jewish settlers living above, but they have started putting up a metal roof over the market. The shuttered shops, doors welded shut, racist graffiti, trashed jewelry district, blocked streets and passages, and windows covered with metal mesh to protect against stones in the Old City all persist. The lower levels of the market flood in the winter with up to four feet of water and garbage. A soldier was videotaped throwing rocks at Palestinians and received a minor punishment. The Jewish yeshiva is expanding and invading into the lives and lands of its Palestinian neighbors, guard towers and cameras are everywhere, and I really mean everywhere. But life goes on. We pass a Palestinian man busily washing his car. There is loud honking and a wedding party; a car decorated with flowers passes by. A computer store is filled with young men glued to their screens.

Hisham takes us through turnstiles and checkpoints to the Tomb of the Patriarchs and the Ibrahimi Mosque and reminds us that Abraham is reported in the Old Testament to have bought the spot for his burial site and the family burial site, but he must have bought it from somebody! This glorious and tortured site has been claimed, rebuilt, invaded, and divided up by all the folks who passed through over the many centuries including Herod, the Romans, the Ottomans, the Crusaders, Saladin, and most recently the Jews. (I am sure I have left somebody out, but you get the point.) And then of course in 1994, after Baruch Goldstein massacred some twenty-nine Muslims and injured 125, the place got divided up between two of the three Abrahamic religions, and the fight continues. We see many more IDF soldiers and a long parade of ultra-orthodox Jews (of the fanatic, fascistic, brown shirt variety), with large families of lovely, innocent-looking children (maybe related to the three yeshiva students?), climbing up the long stairs for Shabbat services. This is when I realize that a committed pacifist like me can harbor outrageously murderous thoughts, but since I have had a lot of therapy, I am clear about the difference between thought and action.

Hisham shows us the checkpoint and metal detector where hundreds of school children have to hustle through every day to get to their classes, the square where three Palestinians were shot to death at different times for the crime of being there. We stare at a man on a donkey loaded with large bundles of straw, yelling and herding a flock of sheep, udders full, up the winding road to get to his side of the street (there are Jewish-only streets and sidewalks around here; I am assuming the sheep are of the Arab persuasion, given the sneer I see pass across the IDF soldier's face). We hear of the fifteen Palestinian families that are so isolated by the maze of walls and barriers that they cannot have visitors and of the incredible challenges families face with the concrete barriers, the front doors they cannot use, the ladders and roof-to-roof alternatives that people take to leave their homes. (Did you get that, roof-to-roof?) But what if you are disabled? Or elderly? Or just bought a bed for your new wife? People die from this kind of life.

It is getting dark and dangerous. I can see the tension in the faces of the young men hanging on the sidewalks, the tone in Hisham's voice; the streets are littered with rocks, the night raids will soon begin, the burning tires, the children dragged out of their beds, the self-righteous cheers and prayers of fanatical Jews with Brooklyn accents and delusions that fill me with shame.

How can I explain this reality to the nice liberal Jews in Brookline or Long Island or Los Angeles who have never really grappled with the long term implications of Zionism, the privileging of Jews over everyone else, whatever the cost and the belief in our perpetual victimhood? This is it, taken to its most extreme, disturbed, and destructive form, and it is heartbreaking, immoral, and outrageous. If we do not speak up, if we do not say "not in my name" and really mean it, I fear it may take us all, Jew and Palestinian, down together.

In the West Bank village of Bil'in, Mohammed Khatib, one of the leaders of the organizing committee for the Friday demonstrations against the separation wall, ongoing land confiscation, and occupation, is wearing a tee shirt that says, "Water and salt = dignity." This is the mantra of the ongoing hunger strike by prisoners largely held in indefinite administrative detention in Israeli jails.

June 21, 2014

There Was No Farewell

Today, Jonathan Cook, a brilliant British journalist and writer now living in Nazareth with a Palestinian wife and family and Israeli citizenship broke my heart. We were wandering through the scattered stones in the cemetery of the destroyed village of Saffuriya, admiring the gorgeous towers of saber cactus, laden with fruit. The saber cactus, (or in Hebrew, *sabra*), is a symbol of indigenous nativeness for both Jews and Palestinians, he explains. For Israelis, the cactus is associated with the return to the land, the creation of the muscular, tough, farmer-Jew deeply rooted in the land, prickly but sweet. For Palestinians, it is a symbol of existence as a resilient indigenous people and of being physically connected to the earth: the cactus was used to denote property boundaries and is virtually impossible to eradicate, so it is a constant reminder of a past that many prefer to forget.

The problem, Jonathan explains gently, is that the saber cactus is not a native plant and was imported from Mexico 350 years ago. Who knew? As proof he notes that Israelis and Palestinians only eat the cactus fruit, while his Mexican friends know how to cook the entire plant because they have done that for centuries.

It is somewhat fitting that my cactus fantasy has come to die in a cemetery. I look around at the jumble of stones and gravesites. It seems that this cemetery is not well maintained, even though the Saffuriyans went to court to obtain the right to care for the site, because they are so harassed by the local *moshavniks* who engage in what Ilan Pappe has termed "memoricide." I think I will stick with the saber/*sabra* mythology out of loyalty to my complicated cactus-loving heritage and in memory of the people buried here.

But I am getting ahead of myself. The main international news I can glean as we drive from Beit Sahour to Nazareth, is that the *New York Times* is now referring to the kidnapping of the yeshiva students as a "disappearance," which sounds like we know even less than before. Hamas is asking Netanyahu for proof that they were involved. Meanwhile, three Palestinians (human beings with mothers and fathers) were killed yesterday and 330 (likely young men, also human) were arrested in the past week. Yesterday in Hebron, the Israeli Defense Forces (twenty- and thirty-somethings, also human with mothers and fathers and trained by one of the most powerful armies in the world), fully armed with the latest in military hardware (most likely), kicked in doors doing house-to-house searches and faced rocks, gasoline bombs, grenades, fireworks, and improvised explosives.

We pass signs to Hebron where the Arabic lettering has been spray painted red (this is a frequent problem with Arabic signage and its deliberate erasure) and see the large red signs at the roads to Palestinian villages and cities warning Israelis not to enter and to beware of the extreme dangers that await them. We drive through a number of checkpoints and are only stopped at one. The soldier (one of five, including a woman who looks fifteen) checks our driver's papers and then opens the van, welcomes me, asks where I am from, wishes me a nice day, and gives me a thumbs up. I restrain myself in the finger department. As we drive north, the streets of Jerusalem are eerily quiet, probably because it is the Sabbath. I keep pondering the idea that the insanity in Hebron—where fanatical Jews, backed by an out of control military, devastate and control a city of Palestinians (who have a right to feel angry)—is not actually deviant behavior; perhaps Hebron can be seen as the vanguard as the Jewish Israeli population becomes dominated politically and demographically by the ultra-right and the painful racist and colonial contradictions of the Zionist dream are revealed. I guess I am still recovering from yesterday.

Jonathan's focus is on the history of Nazareth and Saffuriya and the meaning of the Nakba. He does incredibly careful research and reporting, and I always learn about the nuances and consequences of historical events that are mind-boggling in their complexity. The village of Saffuriya before 1948 consisted of a wide expanse of land (one hundred thousand dunams) with seven thousand people, three mosques, one church, and two schools. In the 1920s it was a leader in the Arab revolt against the British. In the 1930s and 1940s, Jewish soldiers scouted all the Palestinian villages, taking advantage of Arab hospitality, to acquire a detailed database about each town, but they could not get any information about Saffuriya. When the war began, they attacked it early and fiercely. After the bombings, refugees fled to the nearby forests, to Lebanon (Sabra and Shatilla), and to Nazareth; 40% of Nazareth is originally from Saffuriya. When the significance of the refugee crisis became apparent, Jonathan states that Israel asked for a special agency and UNRWA was created with the understanding that no camps would be situated in Israel. (Ah hah moment!) The original village was destroyed (the last structure bulldozed in 1967), and the fenced in area became a closed military zone (shoot on sight-Prevention of Infiltration Law) and Jewish National Forest. Today the rest of the village is the Jewish *moshav* of Zipora.

Jonathan wants us to pay special attention to the trees. This area was once a thickly forested site of pine trees, fast growing and familiar to Jewish Europeans. The trees prevented Palestinians from returning to rebuild, but they also ruined the agricultural land by changing the acidity and destroying the native flora and fauna like nut trees, carobs, citrus, and olives. The trees were thinned out after the massive forest fires: in the 1990s near Ein Hod (a Palestinian village that is now an artist colony with a bar thoughtfully built in the former mosque) and in 2010 with the devastating Haifa-Carmel Fire.

We stop at a field of purple flowers and the original village spring, an area that is now part of Jewish National Fund land, where a Palestinian family is picnicking (staking a claim to their heritage even if only for lunch). The water is supposed to have special powers and is referred to as "Viagra on tap" by some in the *moshav*. The local Palestinians are present absentees, as are 25% of all Palestinians with Israeli citizenship (i.e., present when the state was founded but absent from the property from which they had been expelled. You can't make this stuff up). There is also an archeological site that is controlled by a settler organization. Not only are there Roman ruins here, but this is where Jews fled after the fall of the temple, so there are some who think that the Palestinian villagers of Saffuriya are the original descendants or at least converts from way back then. This is what I love about history! It is so clear.

Jonathan tells us of a Nakba commemoration in 2008 in Saffuriya. Palestinians marched into a nearby forest with their children and their memories because right-wing Jews had taken over the field. In the midst of the commemoration, thuggish police arrived and charged the Palestinians, using tear gas, stun guns and grenades, revealing just how threatening deeply held historical memory can be. This year the Nabka March was enormous, some thirty thousand people celebrated in the town of Lubia, and it was so crowded it lasted for seven hours. This was the first time Jonathan did not feel intimidated, a major psychological breakthrough. The older generation is dying and the young people are reenergizing the event with all the newfangled social media and youthful optimism at their disposal.

We pass through a gate into the *moshav*, which was founded in 1949 for Bulgarian and Rumanian refugees as a dairy farm; this is confirmed by the strong smell of manure. At this point, most members work in the cities and acceptance into the *moshav* is protected by the suitability law that is designed to keep Arabs (as well as gays, disabled folks, single moms, and other undesirables) out of nice Wonder Bread Jewish towns. You know how we feel about racial purity.

We walk along the barbed wire and come across a shrine to the poet Taha Muhammed Ali, the brother of a Nakba survivor we will visit later. Standing in front of the rocks, Jonathan reads us some poetry fragments, softly touching the feelings evoked in such a sad and exquisitely beautiful place:

The Place Itself (extract)*
And so I come to the place itself,
but the place is not
its dust and stones and open space.
For where are the red-tailed birds
and the almonds' green?

---

* Excerpt from "The Place Itself", and "There Was No Farewell" from *So What: New and Selected Poems*, 1971-2005, copyright 2006 by Taha Muhammad Ali, used by permission of Copper Canyon Press, www.coppercanyonpress.org.

Where are the bleating lambs
and pomegranates of evening—
the smell of bread
And the grouse?
Where are the windows,
and where is the ease of Amira's braid?

There Was No Farewell (1988)
We did not weep
When we were leaving—
For we had neither
Time nor tears,
And there was no farewell.
We did not know
at the moment of parting
that it was a parting,
so where would our weeping
have come from?
We did not stay
awake all night
(and did not doze)
the night of our leaving.
That night we had
neither night nor light,
and no moon rose.
That night we lost our star,
our lamp misled us;
we didn't receive our share
Of sleeplessness—
So where
would wakefulness have come from?

Further up the hill is an orphanage run by the Catholic Church
for Palestinian children who are not from Saffuriya. (We don't want
to get any right of return ideas here.) There are lovely geraniums
and cacti, a welcoming Franciscan priest from Venezuela, and a
large ruin, Saint Anna's Church. We are stunned to learn that this
unmarked church, with rows of fallen columns, no roof, ancient

carvings, piteously meowing cats, and a jumble of stones at one end is the birth place of the Virgin Mary!!! Even I, a devout secularist, understand that it is totally weird that this is not a major tourist pilgrimage site. Jonathan thinks that some kind of deal was made between Israel and the Vatican such that the Vatican could keep the church and the orphanage but no pilgrims would be encouraged because then they would see the destroyed village and barbed wire and ask annoying questions. Three schlumpy people arrive, but they are Russians from Haifa and do not seem that impressed by the Virgin. The Israelis also will not issue a permit to restore the church or at least put a roof over the site for protection. Got to love religion. The only surviving house in Saffuriya is now a B&B with a big Israeli flag.

We are now heading to Nazareth Illit (the word means "above" but also implies some moral superiority). The mayor erected some ginormous Israeli flags as a clear message that he intends to keep out the Arabs. Now this history is messy and confusing. The main points are that in the 1950s, our friend David Ben Gurion announced the Judaization of the Galilee with some comment to the effect, "Why so many Arabs?" They were supposed to have been run out during the war. The focus was on Nazareth, the only successful, thriving Palestinian city that could potentially become a cultural and political force. So he confiscated thousands of acres of Nazareth (lovely man, that David Ben Gurion) and built a Jewish neighborhood and a resorption center for incoming Jewish refugees, while the Palestinians in the city below lived under military rule, and the Israeli Defense Forces built an army of Palestinian collaborators through various devious ways with a desperate population.

The goals of Judaization are to contain, isolate, and fragment the Palestinian community, so Nazareth Illit is shaped like an octopus, and the surrounding villages have never coalesced into a political or cultural force. The next goal is to redirect resources from Palestinian citizens to Jewish citizens, so the imposing administrative offices were built on land confiscated from guess who; this is ringed by a road also annexed to Nazareth Illit. The Israeli army annexed land as well, and the fancy Plaza Hotel was built in Nazareth Illit to capture tourist dollars from Nazareth, which I will remind you is a very important religious site. Then there are the

industrial areas also annexed to Nazareth Illit (including, unfortunately, a delicious chocolate factory). You get the pattern. The final
goal was to build a system of surveillance on hilltops, which let's
just say happened in spades.

The Israeli legal system kicked in with a variety of laws and rul-
ings that recognized only 124 of the 204 Palestinian villages still in
Israel, determined the blue lines for city expansion (Jewish towns
get a lot, Palestinian towns get nothing beyond the 1965 boundaries
and can only build up to four stories), communities can use compatibility laws to keep out Arabs, and no one in the Jewish cities
will sell to a Palestinian family. And the list goes on and is quite
disgusting, I must say, especially since we are talking about the only
democracy in the Middle East.

The mayor of Nazareth Illit, after describing Nazareth as a "nest
of terror," had difficulties attracting new residents, but he lucked
out when one million Russians arrived looking for a place to live.
Now, immigration is at a standstill; Russians who want to get out
of this less-than-desirable place are willing to sell to middle class
Palestinians who cannot find housing in Nazareth. The clever
mayor, seeing that 20% of Nazareth Illit is now Arab, has morphed
the absorption center into a hesder yeshiva, a center for orthodox
Torah study and military preparation, in other words, a real nest
of terror (finally!). Oh and he has also invited right-wing settlers
originally from Gaza and other West Bank settlements to move
in. And for extra credit, he is building a neighborhood of three
thousand only for *Haredim* families, thus creating tension between
the religious and the secular, so there are now modesty patrols,
women attacked with acid, and shops burned, and we are not in
Tehran (yet). This makes the modern Christian Palestinians with
their short sleeves and tight jeans wonder if it is time to leave.
Interestingly, the mayor is under indictment for corruption, but he
was still elected in a landslide.

While this all may seem a bit crazy, the important concept here
is that this whole exercise is about Judaization, getting rid of the
Palestinians and creating a Jewish state by any means necessary,
and that is the fundamental flaw of Zionism as it is now practiced.
This is not a sustainable model for Jews or for Palestinians; trying to
make everything "Jewish" (whatever that means, and I would argue
that most of what I have described is far from "Jewish" but falls

under topic headers like racist, prejudiced, Islamophobic, ignorant, etc.) and is not what the richness and grand multiculturalism of life is all about. It also is not a good strategy to protect against anti-Semitism which exists in the world. As Jonathan explains, it "turns us into monsters." Nazareth and its big sister are just a microcosm of this growing national tragedy.

Can You Be an Israeli Citizen and What Does That Mean Anyway?

I know Jonathan Cook explained this last year, but the topic is so contorted and bizarre I am going to give it another try and forgive me if it is not crystal clear. We are sitting in the charming Al Mutran Guest House surrounded by glass cases of embroidery and pottery in what was once a Palestinian home, with patios and garden on the second floor, serene views, puffy clouds. Looks can be deceiving. I notice that a hulky four-wheel drive vehicle has actually driven up the stone stairs to park in front of the guest house at a 45 degree angle, either out of desperation for a parking space or perhaps because Nazareth is a place of angels and miracles and unimaginable possibility.

So one of the first dilemmas facing the new State of Israel (after giving all the Jews in the world the Law of Return, which entitles them to Israeli citizenship and theoretically a safe place from anti-Semitism) is how to know if a non-Jewish Arab type person is a present absentee/refugee from 1948 or an "infiltrator" who has snuck back in to harvest olives, retrieve belongings, take revenge, etc., etc. The "kosher" Palestinians were given residency and, in 1952, official citizenship, but since Ben Gurion and his friends are building a Jewish state here, the other goal is to limit the number of Palestinian citizens in any way possible.

So here, according to Jonathan, are some of the more quirky facts:

1. If an Israeli citizen (who is "Arab") wants to marry a sweetheart from the occupied territories, since the Oslo Accords in 1993, it is almost impossible for said sweetheart

to get Israeli citizenship. If an Israeli Palestinian (there is no satisfactory word for this category) applies for naturalization for his/her spouse, the process can take five years, and when it is not successful, there is a legal challenge, which can go to the high court. In 1999, the court ruled that said spouse should get citizenship, so the Israeli government passed the 2003 Citizenship and Residency Laws, which froze all applications and has basically functionally banned marriage across the Green Line. Remember the goal is not to allow one more Palestinian to become an Israeli citizen by any means possible!

2. In Britain, Jonathan was a British national and British citizen, but in Israel there are 137 (yes 1-3-7) nationalities and the courts have agreed twice that citizenship and nationality are different and confer different rights. (Get a cup of coffee and read this really slowly.) Nationality (for example: Jewish is a nationality) trumps citizenship because it is very important that all the citizens of Israel should not be legally equal in a Jewish state, so this factoid is the key to institutionalized discrimination. So after a long administrative battle, Jonathan became an Israeli citizen with British nationality, made possible because he has a wife with Arab nationality and Israeli citizenship. To make things even more confusing, on Israeli passports (don't want to look bad at passport control in JFK), nationality is written as Israeli, but on the Israeli ID that everyone must have, nationality is listed as *****. Yes, that is a row of stars. I saw Jonathan's ID card. The star ship identity is a consequence of the big debate over WHO IS REALLY A JEW. The state uses the Nazi definition (sort of poetic justice) that if you have one Jewish grandparent, then by law you are a Jew. But the Orthodox rabbinate, which controls much of civic and personal law, uses the you-got-to-have-a-Jewish-mother rule. This is a major social and political nightmare and headache.

In the 1990s, one million Russians arrive in Israel and 350,000 are not Jewish, or they are what are called "grey Jews." Confused?

So nice Russian Jewish man marries nice Russian Christian lady and they arrive in Tel Aviv with their four lovely children. By state law, the man and his children are Jews, by religious law only the man is a Jew. This is critical because, for example, the non-Jewish (or sort of Jewish) children cannot marry as Jews in Israel because all Jewish marriages are ONLY done by Orthodox rabbis, there is no civil marriage. (Hence the quick wedding in Cyprus.) So there was a big fight about what nationality to put on their Israeli ID cards and the court agreed that a row of ***** was a good solution. The underlying motivation as I have said is to limit non-Jews and to keep resources and privileges flowing to the Jews rather than to everyone else.

When the Ethiopian Jews were "rescued" and airlifted "home" they were not considered Jewish enough by the Israeli rabbinate and so they had to (re)convert to Judaism, which is a challenging process and also involves a commitment to sending your children to religious schools, where they will study Torah but skip science, literature, multiculturalism, etc., etc. Factoid: the educational ministry recently ruled that evolution MUST be taught in all Israeli schools, which implies that it was not before the ruling.

But it is not that simple (not that it was simple in the first place). A knowledgeable person can tell if someone is a Jew by their ID number, by their father's and grandfather's names listed on the card, or if the date of birth is in the Hebrew or Gregorian calendar. Pretty sneaky if you ask me.

We are all a bit cross-eyed at this point, but Jonathan continues. Israel has two fundamental sets of rights: the core rights related to citizenship and the rights related to nationality. Nationality always trumps citizenship. There are currently fifty-seven laws that institutionally discriminate against non-Jews and the discrimination is so entrenched it is invisible to most of the folks who love Israel as a symbol of Jewish redemption and justice.

So examples:

1. Immigration: Jews can come anytime; Palestinians are totally unwelcome in an endless variety of ways.
2. Water: Water is a core right but its allocation and cost are related to the nationality of the recipient. Palestinians in Area C (the part of the West Bank totally

under Israeli control; remember the occupier is responsible for the welfare of the occupied? But that is another story.) are not entitled to water because they are not citizens of Israel, while Moishe who is watering his lawn in the settlement next door gets lots of water because he is a citizen. Palestinians in general pay much more for water. Water is subsidized by the state if it is used for agricultural or farming practices like in *kibbutizim* or *moshavim*, which by definition are only for Jews. At some point, I think in response to Land Day (the commemoration of March 30, 1976 when thousands of Palestinians with Israeli citizenship protested the expropriation of their land in the Galilee; six were killed and thousands injured and jailed), Palestinians were allowed to keep some of their farmland but not allocated any agricultural water, so they are forced to grow olive trees, which are highly drought resistant. If they do not farm for three years, then the land is officially "fallow" and seized by the state.

3. Land: 93% of the land in Israel is nationalized for Jewish use only and controlled by the Israel Land Authority (80%) and the Jewish National Fund (13%). If a Jew "buys" land, it is actually a ninety-nine year lease that can be passed on to future generations. The family is the "guardian" of the Jewish land. Palestinians can't do this, obviously.

Jonathan argues that in Israel, nationality is really what the rest of us think of as citizenship and citizenship is really more like residency. Nationality is the only thing that really counts, and Jews from Beijing to Buenos Aires are all potential members of this nation state. Everyone else is treated more like (temporary) residents who just happen to be passing through and hopefully will leave real soon.

But alas, Ben Gurion's dream of an Arab-rein state is not fulfilled, and after Oslo, Palestinians with Israeli citizenship begin to pay more attention to that citizenship thing. Azmi Bishara, a Palestinian Knesset member, founds a party called Balad and introduces a fascinating concept: A state for all its citizens. In 2006,

Prime Minister Olmert meets with his buddies in the Shin Bet and issues a statement that this concept constitutes subversion and that the State of Israel will use any means necessary, including non-democratic means to foil this plan. Bishara leaves the country and is informed that if he returns he will be tried for treason. I think he is now in Qatar or somewhere, working as a journalist. So think about this: When Palestinians say (as if they actually believe in democracy) that they want equal citizenship, this is considered subversion or treason. In the United States we call this state of affairs institutionalized, legal discrimination, Jim Crow, or apartheid. In Israel we call this normal.

Memory Keeper

I first met Abu Arab and his museum of artifacts from destroyed villages last year. Jonathan warns us to be respectful and to remember that "this is his Holocaust." Abu Arab, a tall man with thick greying hair and a twinkle in his eye, recognizes me and greets me with a warm handshake and smile. First we wander among old, dusty farming equipment, pedal-powered sewing machines, tattered clothes, rows of pots of multiple sizes, a cross between a museum and a cemetery holding a life gone by. Listening to his story reminds me of the speak bitterness talks I first heard from elderly Chinese women in the 1970s and from a host of subsequent traumatized people from all over the world. I think of Edward Said's words to the effect that people survive by telling their stories. I remember Herzl's comments about Palestinians (he probably said Arabs), "No culture, no folklore, no heritage." What did he know?

Abu Arab was born in the vibrant town of Saffuriya in 1935; he remembers a time of peaceful relations between Arab and Jew. His family were peasants and fled in 1948. They were attacked during Ramadan, bombed by two aircraft, 80% of the seven thousand villagers fled, mostly north to Lebanon. After twenty-eight days, they were taken by the Red Cross to Beirut, and then to a village in Syria, but ultimately returned to their village. There is a quiet intensity to his voice, which rises with indignation, hands gesturing for emphasis. Months later, the villagers received ID cards and months after that were advised to leave in forty-eight hours or be shot. They were told to remove all the furniture from their homes and their possessions were confiscated. The villagers appealed to the courts; they had IDs denoting place of birth (Saffuriya), place of residence (Saffuriya), occupation (farmer). Over the course of five months, eighty villagers were killed, shot while collecting food for their families. Some ten Jewish settlements and *moshavim* were built on the bulldozed site.

Abu Arab wants recognition of this crime and the right of return for internal and external refugees. He states this conflict is all about land; it is a struggle against Zionism, not Jews. He advises us: "Tell the truth, do what is good." School children come here to learn the stories of their grandparents and to understand that these discarded artifacts are actually the treasures documenting rural life. I can imagine the village women cooking and embroidering, the families collecting olives, the collections of sisters and brothers and cousins playing in the fields. I am always impressed by the simple humanity and dignity held in Abu Arab's memories and words.

In the past few years, I have heard so many of these narratives and pored over hundreds of historical photos in the course of making my own documentary film, "Voices Across the Divide," my contribution to telling and owning the story of the Nakba. I have come to understand that this history is not only a tragedy for the Palestinians, but the ethnic cleansing of Palestine is an integral part of the history of the creation of the State of Israel, just as much as the history of Native Americans or African slaves is part of US history. There is no "dual narrative" here. The Nakba is not an alternative history; it is the narrative that is invisible in Israeli society and the textbooks for all Israeli children, Palestinian and Jew. It is a story that must be heard.

Abu Arab was born in 1935 and fled under attack in 1948 from Saffuriya, a vibrant village of one hundred thousand dunams, seven thousand people, three mosques, one church, and two schools. He collects artifacts from destroyed villages to keep the memory of the past alive (fighting "memoricide") and to create a just resolution to the losses suffered by the Palestinian population.

June 22, 2014

Zochrot: Bending the Arc towards Justice

So why should Jewish Israelis care about what happened to the people they defeated 67 years ago? The Arabs rejected the Partition Plan, there was a war (they started it), we won, *yalla*, move on. That is what I call the dominant paradigm in both Israel and the United States. Eitan Bronstein, founder of an organization called Zochrot (Remembering) is a little older and little greyer than when I last saw him but still driven by the need to bring the history of the Nakba, the Palestinian experience of 1948, into Israeli consciousness. His intensity and conviction is powerful. I am pleased to see he has a new office that reflects the growing success and activities of the organization.

In 2001, he was touring a Jewish National Forest and noted that while there were signs about Roman ruins and biblical sites and Mamluks, there was no documentation of an obviously neglected Palestinian village, Imwas. "The houses were shouting to me," the cemetery, the stones, "like an obvious blindness." He was working with Neve Shalom/Wahat Salaam, the only consciously Jewish-Palestinian village devoted to coexistence in Israel, talked with his friend Umar, and they decided to put up signs reflecting the more recent history. This got picked up by a journalist, there was an article in *kibbutz* newspapers, then a list of Palestinian villages on sites of *kibbutzim*. Tom Segev wrote about this in a column in the Israeli newspaper *Haaretz*, and the idea took off.

Eitan explains that this work "has to do with my own colonizer identity, signage is colonizing practicing." As Ben Gurion said, "In 1948, we took over the land, now we have to take over the map." Eitan states, "Our way to de-colonize is to rename." He sees the mission of Zochrot is to educate Israeli Jews and civil society about the Nakba and the more controversial right of return for Palestinian refugees, and to take responsibility for the Nakba. This is not just Palestinian history, it is Israeli and human history, "part of my own history."

There are many invisible pieces to this puzzle. According to Eitan, the 1948 war did not happen between two sides where there was a winner and a loser; the war was mainly between Jewish Israeli fighters and Arab armies, not the local civilians on the ground. Israel lost some of the battles when they encountered an Arab army: the Old City of Jerusalem, or the region of Latrun, but many of the victories were over civilians who were not prepared to do battle. Additionally, the Nakba happened before the war, during the war, and after the war. He finds the most convincing evidence is the testimonies of Israeli fighters: "Expulsions were easy, shoot a few shots, tell people to leave; it was not a military challenge from the thousands of Palestinians." So he sees this history as a systematic expulsion of a civilian population by armed units followed by the destruction of their villages to prevent return, thus the Nakba continues. He adds that this is not the Israeli understanding of history; most now know the word Nakba, but most people do not really comprehend its meaning.

To complicate matters, the Israeli government passed the Nakba Law in 2011, which creates financial sanctions for any commemoration of the Nakba by an organization funded by the state. On Israeli Independence Day a Jewish state should celebrate, not mourn! This creates an atmosphere of fear and threats around the commemoration of the Nakba. On the other hand, the law raised a lot of interest. There was a huge scandal over an earlier law that actually said that anyone who commemorated the Nakba on Israeli Independence Day could be sent to jail for one year. Fortunately this did not pass. Eitan explains, imagine if the United States forbade any mourning or protest by Native Americans on July 4th or Thanksgiving. Even Australians remember the day they attacked and massacred the aboriginal population.

Since Zochrot is not funded by the state, it is still a legal, functioning organization. Universities are also closed on Independence Day, so students do not organize commemorations. Two years ago, students at Tel Aviv University initiated a provocative commemoration on Nakba Day which raised a lot of attention and a big argument in the media. The university permitted the event, but the government said this was not okay because it violated the spirit of the Nakba Law, which was to prevent all such events. At this point, Nakba commemorations occur on May 15th, the day Israel declared independence, but the national independence day celebrations occur according to the Hebrew calendar, so the days are usually not the same.

I find it an interesting historical point that while most Palestinians in Israel lived under military rule until 1966, i.e., they needed permits to travel within Israel, this rule was lifted on Independence Day, and no permits were needed. So on that day, Palestinian families for years would visit their villages for personal, mostly quiet, less political family gatherings. Fifteen years ago, they held their first March of Return on Israeli Independence Day, so the issue is becoming increasingly politicized and public and Zochrot is in the forefront of this struggle.

Zochrot is involved in a number of extraordinary projects:

1. Offering alternative tours like the one we did to the destroyed village of Lifta.
2. Creating the only Hebrew map of destroyed Palestinian villages.
3. Documenting all the destroyed villages since the beginning of Zionism through the 1967 war and placing 678 localities, including 22 Jewish localities destroyed in 1948 by Arab armies and 62 Palestinian localities destroyed before 1948. Eitan explains that when Zionists "redeemed the land," they destroyed the Arab structures. Landowners were sometimes Palestinian, Lebanese, or other large, often absentee, landowners. Eitan was told that the Golan was empty and only had Syrian army bases there, but Zochrot documented 127 Syrian villages with approximately 170,000 people.
4. Preparing an educational study guide for high schools. While they cannot get officially invited to schools, they train teachers to use their material and to include the information in their lessons. While teachers can get fired and have been bureaucratically threatened,

Zochrot advises them to be "discreet," to introduce the idea of "multiple narratives." This reality obviously poisons the atmosphere for many teachers who want to explore this topic in depth.

5. Writing a very successful, practical tour guide in Hebrew and Arabic, with eighteen routes to different places in the Nakba with photos, maps, and history.

6. Creating a book called *Awda* (Return) with imagined testimonies for possible futures after the right of return for Palestinian refugees is implemented. There are twelve stories, six by Jews and six by Palestinians.

7. Creating an iNakba app for iPhones, a free download that uses GPS, and accurately shows all villages, photos, and related information.

8. And facilitating a host of educational workshops, symposiums, film festivals, websites, and coalitions with other groups such as Badil, Al Haq, and Palestinians in the West Bank, Lebanon, Syria, as well as Israel.

Zochrot's most controversial work, I suspect, is on the right of return for Palestinian refugees. Eitan explains, "We support the right of return based on the right to choose or to compensate with reparations; it is the choice of the refugees." How to actualize this is a very big challenge, it is clearly not practical for people to expect to return to their old homes, often places are not there, some are vacant, or now encompass a different community. "We try to show how implementation is not putting us in more danger and will actually favor peace and prosperity." He is not talking about symbolic numbers, like the Geneva Initiative and other agreements. "We do not accept that ideology," and as an example he explains: in practical terms, find out how many people want to return. "So let's say here are one million Jaffa refugees, maybe one hundred thousand may return. How do we do that, so we must prepare to absorb these folks, so when, how, time frame (one million Russians came, it takes time)."

He continues on that he favors a one-state solution, where everyone can live in equality, where the state is no longer a Jewish state. "This is the core reason of the conflict and is very problematic. In the context of the Mideast, this is a good recipe for constant war. We already have a big Israeli collective here, a culture. Hebrew speakers will continue and be enriched by Arabs. Everyone should be bilingual, why not? We are in the Mideast; Jewish tradition and culture will continue but not as a state."

So how did Eitan come to such an idealistic, and some might consider radical, position? "We began right after the onset of the Second Intifada, a crisis of the left." In October 2000, he had, "My last crisis with Zionism. I finally understood that the problem is Zionism. Many more Israelis are exposed to this knowledge," but they are still a minority. Many Israelis acknowledge the Nakba, but cannot deal with the right of return, but "it is not possible to dismiss." Thinking back to the hundreds of children we saw playing in the barren concrete streets of the Balata and Aida Refugee Camps and the massive security apparatus and concrete walls that the Israeli government and military continue to erect in their increasingly ghettoized efforts to protect themselves, it is clear that it is time to think beyond the dominant paradigm, and Zochrot is clearly a good place to start.

Crying and Shooting

We have not had enough sleep in days and are suffering from that weariness that comes with bearing witness to injustices that seem overwhelming, over and over again, and standing in solidarity with people who have no other choice but to get up and do it again. Ronnie Barkan, a friendly, energetic, probably early thirties Israeli joins us for lunch in Jaffa at a hangout known for its excellent salads and spicy political conversation. A member of Boycott from Within and Anarchists Against the Wall, he is like a bolt of rapid fire inspiration and provocative ideas. We all celebrate the historic decision by the Presbyterian Church in the United States to divest from three companies that support the mechanics of occupation: Hewlett Packard, Motorola, and Caterpillar, and then dive into the hummus and eggplant and an intense historical and political discussion. Ronnie explains that as a young teen he struggled with his impending mandatory army service. "You know we are prepared for the army since kindergarten"; he did not want to be "a parasite," as Israelis refer to refusers, and then there was Avigdor Lieberman's "no duties, no rights." He got drafted and during the first two months, he decided he could no longer eat meat. A week later he decided to leave the military, "My only obligation was to humanity." He waited one and a half years in the military, doing very little, occasional office work, doctor's appointments, but his superior would not send him to jail. The endless limbo and waiting felt like a terrible punishment.

He is quite clear that there is no Israeli left, no peace camp, and that the core issue is the refusal of liberal Zionists who really are good people, support human rights and equality, etc., but are unable to face the facts of 1948 and the implications of the creation of a Jewish state. Many folks are ready to end the occupation, and may even acknowledge the Nakba, but discussing full equality for Palestinians and the right of return for millions of refugees created as a consequence of the 1948 war is unthinkable and deeply threatening. The big crisis facing folks who actually believe in democracy is that Jews are now no longer the majority in the land Israel controls, "from the river to the sea," so Israelis are facing the uncomfortable idea that a shrinking minority of Jews will be ruling a growing majority of non-Jews. That is increasingly hard to justify and looks really bad in the international community, of which Israel wants to be a part. Ronnie finds folks in AIPAC (the right-wing American Israel Public Affairs Committee) refreshing because at least they are honest and sometimes even proud of their racism. It is easier to argue with them! Yes the ethnic cleansing happened, it was absolutely necessary for the survival of the Jewish people, and the only big problem is that we haven't finished the job. Okay, now we know where everyone stands.

Ronnie describes Israel matter-of-factly as an apartheid state, a system based on one racial-ethnic group oppressing another. He sees the Israeli courts as the main vehicle of apartheid; he sees Zionism as fundamentally racist and supremacist, and the country profoundly undemocratic for all of these reasons. He finds the argument that we must work to protect Israeli democracy, "a discourse of lies," because there never was a democracy. "It is impossible to be both moral and Zionist." His clarity is refreshing; his absolutism and style reminds me of white male activists from my student movement days: very politically correct but unaware of their white male and, in this case, Ashkenazic privilege; women, Sephardim, nuance, and gradual political growth are not part of his discourse. On the other hand, I understand his utter frustration with Israeli politics.

Between pita and pickled beets, mint lemonade, and warm falafel, we listen intently, questioning, asking for clarification. He cites the expression: "shooting and crying," i.e., the comment made by some famous Israeli (was it Golda Meir?) that, "We will forgive the Arabs for killing *our* children but we will never forgive the Arabs for making *us* kill *their* children." How did we ever blame the victim for our crimes? He recommends a book by an early Matzpen member, *The Un-Jewish State*, and tells us the story of the first Jewish political assassination, which happened pre-1948 when an orthodox Jew who was anti-Zionist discussed the idea of living together as equals with the King of Jordan. This kind of thinking was profoundly threatening to the Zionist movement and the guy was killed.

Ronnie reviews the recent law that requires ultra-Orthodox yeshiva students to serve in the army, "to share the burden"; they need to fill their quota of bodies ready to defend the state. This is seen by many ultra-Orthodox as an attack by the state on the religion of Judaism; in a sense criminalizing the study of Torah at the altar of Zionism. (Is he in sympathy with the ultra-Orthodox? Are they the definers of Judaism? What about their treatment of women or their racism towards Arabs?) This law has also served as a rallying cry to unite the many different sectors of ultra-Orthodoxy into a unified block, much of it anti-Zionist and not interested in being modernized and molded into a nationalistic Israeli macho man. I am starting to see those photos of tens of thousands of black-hatted men in Jerusalem rallying against the draft in a (very slightly) more sympathetic light.

Ronnie is an optimistic kind of guy; in 2005, the boycott, divestment, and sanctions movement (BDS) was not in the public discourse and now even Kerry mumbled the words as he flummoxed around the broken "peace process" and for the first time in history suggested that the Israelis might be at fault. BDS is now affecting churches, businesses, and, perhaps most importantly, cultural and academic events. Ronnie works with groups of activists who write letters and petitions to churches and artists, pressures performers to avoid coming to Israel, researches companies profiting from the occupation, creates educational events. There is no neutral position in this battle. Music may be a universal language, but performing in a large hall in Tel Aviv is a political statement. This is not a normal situation. Despite the small numbers, BDS is finally part of the public and intellectual discourse; the national fight against the BDS movement is now organized by the Ministry of Strategic Affairs, who also deal with the other big enemy of Israel: Iran!

While Ronnie sees political change happening, he feels the struggle really is not centered in Israel but rather the European Union and the United States, and he is leaving to work in Europe, hoping to piece his activism together with some IT, web building, teaching, some way to support himself while trying to change the world. He feels that once apartheid ends (*insha'allah*), then it will be time to work within a multicultural Israeli society, to build just and democratic institutions and to learn to live together as equals despite the differences that drive people apart. I love his youthful optimism. His absolutist political style makes me wonder if he ever goes beyond the choir or if that is even his goal.

Now, as we sip our final cup of thick coffee, two conscientious objectors sit in Israeli jails and another 20 high school students, *shministim*, have signed a letter stating their objections to serving in the military. NBC is producing a major extravaganza called DIG, partially financed by the Israeli Ministry of Trade. The series is focusing on archeology in Israel-Palestine, particularly in Silwan, where Palestinians are being dispossessed and a profoundly politicized sham of archeologists are setting out to prove the existence of the City of David. (The Jews were here first theory of archeology.) They were filming in Jaffa last week and Ronnie was there, disrupting the set, causing a fuss, calling attention to the propaganda disguised as education and entertainment. They did not arrest him, he explains, as that did not fit the script. Maybe next time.

"What do I know?
I am just a Bedouin?" A Lot.

My glasses (somewhat symbolically) have broken; perhaps my brain does not want to see any more, but there is so much to witness. Even with my eyes closed I can hear the military jets overhead as we drive towards the unrecognized Bedouin village of Alsira in the *Naqab* (Negev). My old emergency glasses leave me with a headache, double vision, and a sense that the world I am experiencing is intensely out of focus, which in reality it is.

Khalil al-Amour greets us and invites us up to his shaded patio for water and juice. He has a sun-browned, open face with laughing eyes and a quirky sense of humor. He points to the demolition order glued on his door, dated September 2006. It is addressed, "To the house owner," has no checks next to the list of grievances, and is signed by some official who clearly cannot distinguish one Bedouin from another. The form is a photocopy. Khalil is a math and computer teacher and just received his law degree. He works with Adalah, a legal group that advocates for Bedouin rights in Israel, and he is leaving soon for Geneva for a UN conference on the rights of indigenous peoples. He is busy preparing for his son's wedding and for the upcoming month of Ramadan. Have I challenged any of your preconceptions yet?

Clothespins clip a map of the *Naqab* onto the grating over a front window where rows of socks are also drying. Khalil explains that Bedouins used to live in the entire *Naqab*, thirteen million dunams (approximately three and a quarter million acres). They had no major problems during four hundred years of Ottoman control and thirty years of the British mandate and then came 1948. Ninety thousand were expelled, most fleeing to the Egyptian Sinai desert, some went to Jordan, and eleven thousand remained. The Israelis "relocated" them to an area called the Siyag, a fenced in reservation and closed military zone. The Bedouin were traumatized by the massive expulsion and by the confiscation of 90% of their land. The Israelis kept shrinking the land available to the Bedouin and expanding the southern city of Be'ersheba. They took eighty thousand dunams to build a huge military airport nearby.

I start counting the number of planes roaring overhead. More Jewish cities were built in the area, but the Bedouin stayed and married and made babies, so now there are more than two hundred thousand. "We are a big surprise." The Prawer Plan (a plan to dispossess the remaining Bedouin and transfer them to townships) is currently frozen, but it will undoubtedly resurface in that bastion of justice, the Knesset, and squeeze the population, which represents 30% of the *Naqab,* into 2% of the land. Dimona, the Israeli nuclear reactor (the one that Israel has officially denied for decades) is located in the southeast area of the proposed relocations. (Health hazards anyone?)

Khalil remarks in a disconcertingly cheerful manner, "It really drives me crazy sometimes. Most Israelis are very stupid, listen to the media, the lies. How do we have these smart people, Jewish people are not stupid, [but] their behavior towards Bedouin and minorities is very strange. I expect more understanding with the Holocaust.... And it is worse and worse."

Bedouin have repeatedly rejected efforts to push them into poverty-stricken, crime-ridden townships. "We are not good friends with cities!" Khalil explains, "I am half Polish and half Bedouin!" His daughter interrupts for his iPhone. He explains that he was studying in Be'ersheba at the teacher's college and sleeping in the park. A gas station offered him a part-time job, but it was not enough money for rent as his family was very poor. He laughs and says this Polish couple who had lost their own child, adopted him and took care of him for three years. As they got older, Khalil took care of them until they died and then he returned to his village.

His son is a physiotherapist, studied in Jordan, works in Be'ersheba, but returns home every day. Another son is studying medicine in Moldova, but he will also return. "We love the desert, this is our life." He explains that not only does he have a demolition order on his house, but also on his animal bins and his generator. The orders are created from an aerial map and he is #67. He remarks ironically that being #67 reminds him of the Holocaust. "Nazi is a behavior. They created this regime." Khalil has good Jewish friends who also get very angry.

He explains that there are forty-five unrecognized villages; every one of them is named; some are new, some are old. The Israelis took the fertile lands; Ariel Sharon had a large ranch in the *Naqab.* The

Bedouin have limited access to water, pay very high rates, have no electricity, no nearby schools or clinics. We drove into the town partly on the road to the airport. "We paved the road, connected to the water system, made solar energy, established two daycares for the children. We take care of ourselves."

In the townships, they are offered high mortgages and a small plot of land (remember this is a traditional agricultural society with goats, cows, and sheep to herd). He says this township life is particularly hard for the women. They can't make cheese, can't do their traditional farming, can't weave rugs. "They have no value." They are given a microwave and washing machine (Israelis talk of modernization and improved living standards) and are "humiliated, no respect."

"We have lived marginalized and neglected, no problem, we can live the next sixty years. They won't even let us do that. Let the Bedouin live." He takes us on an extraordinary tour of his property and at every stop he smiles and explains how much he loves his solar panels, loves his chickens, loves his mulberries, olives, sage, fresh eggs, the man is deeply in love with the land he lives with and he is deeply happy. His friends thought he was crazy, but he researched on the internet and learned how to set up solar panels; his friends were finally convinced when they noticed his refrigerator was working twenty-four hours per day. He traveled to Canada and the United States (even went to Las Vegas and is happy he does not smoke, gamble, or drink) to learn about solar energy.

Every year he would make fifty liters of olive oil from his trees, but he noticed they were dying from lack of water. Back to the internet and YouTube and he developed an ingenious system for collecting grey water with pipes, collecting tanks, pumps, and filters, providing drip irrigation to his rejuvenated trees. He is beaming as he shows us the lush clusters of happy olives. "I am not a genius, I am regular." But he loves his chickens and scoops up three eggs; he eats two fresh eggs every morning and assures us that he only feeds the birds natural grains. We look across the brown rolling desert to the huge military area where he used to go to school and where his people used to bury their dead. He recently visited for the first time in thirty-two years with a group that went to maintain the cemetery.

And then he is back picking white mulberries for us (the taste is a cross between blackberries and strawberries). He remarks that he traveled to the United States with the Tree of Life Conference and laughs, "I was almost converted to Christianity!" He was hosted by Christians and Jews. We look up at the antennae for his phone and internet and the router attached to the corner of his house. He jokes that a bird sometimes nests there and so he also has Twitter. As we leave his house he points to a large collection of ants and he assures us (cheerfully) that he never kills them. "They were here before me." Apparently they are coexisting quite successfully.

We wander through the dry dusty neighborhood, women are cleaning, cooking, children scatter about; there are manually rotating solar panels, a "white house" for community gatherings and celebrations, other homes of varying sturdiness. The village put up an ironic sign denoting the location of the town. In Arabic it says "Alsira," the English is misspelled as "Alsra," and in Hebrew it says, "Established in the Ottoman Empire." Like I said, the guy has a sense of humor. Below the sign is a triangular warning sign, again tongue in cheek, with a house and a bulldozer, warning the hapless visitor that they are now entering a demolition zone. Such dangerous, uneducated, unimaginative people these Bedouins!

This village has no sheikh, but rather a local committee of five people that provides leadership. There are two big clans and five family groups representing seventy individual families and over one hundred children. There is also a Regional Council of Unrecognized Villages. There are no women in leadership, but two that are very active. Khalil reminds us that this is a conservative community, there is some polygamy, but "I am an open minded guy." Nowadays girls do not get married before eighteen.

Last year, our delegation visited the village of Al Araqib, north of Be'ersheba. Khalil explains this village has "the saddest story," which includes expulsion in 1948, repeated land confiscations, returning to the village, Israeli military spraying fields and animals with Round Up, multiple legal cases, repeated demolitions. (See my blog posts from 2013.) Last year, the villagers were living in the cemetery, "First time in history the dead people protect the live ones," and the Jewish National Fund had planted the Ambassador Forest on their agricultural land, rows of water hungry eucalyptus trees. Last week, the Israeli forces demolished everything in the cemetery, approximately the 70th demolition. Now the villagers are under the trees, using blankets for cover, they are "upset and nervous," and the sheikh, who was "warm and happy," is feeling "angry." Rabbi Arik Ascherman from Rabbis for Human Rights was arrested at the cemetery site and the demolitions have attracted attention from international NGOs and the UN.

Khalil asserts, "Our voice will be heard." In the past, a delegation of Native Americans came and wrote an urgent letter to the Israelis. "I am optimistic. We don't have the privilege to give up. This is racism."

The twelfth military plane screeches overhead, breaking the desert silence.

As we drive back to Ramallah passing near Hebron, we see Israeli forces marching with flags in some kind of military formation; we see a group of soldiers breaking into a house, our eyes burn from tear gas wafting from the city. Later we learn that Palestinians have been killed in Nablus, Hebron, and Ramallah where an Israeli sniper shot an unarmed man watching from a rooftop. Later that night the Israeli Defense Forces conduct an incursion into Ramallah (remember Area A under control by the Palestinian Authority???) in front of the Palestinian Authority (PA) police station; the PA does nothing to protect its people (it is in obvious collusion with the IDF), and when the IDF leaves, the enraged crowd attacks the police station and the PA attacks the crowd.

The media and the streets are filled with stories about the missing boys (Yeshiva students? Armed right-wing settlers? Paramilitary? Everyone has a theory) and Netanyahu's blind rage. The entire Palestinian population in the West Bank and Gaza is under attack because three young men are missing, because Hamas and Fatah are talking, because the farce of the peace process has been laid bare, because, well because they are here and they are Palestinian. And that, it seems, is a crime in itself.

Eitan Bronstein, founder of Zochrot, is committed to finding creative ways to teach Israelis about the Nakba and the invisible Palestinian experience before, during, and after 1948 as well as the right of return. Located in Tel Aviv, Zochrot has developed educational materials, corrective signage, and tours, and here, Eitan is demonstrating the new iNakba app, a free download that uses GPS and accurately shows all destroyed villages, photos, and related information.

June 23, 2014

Tarnishing the Israeli Brand

Our meeting with Omar Barghouti, one of the leaders of the Boycott, Divestment, and Sanctions (BDS) movement, starts in a stairwell, since the office where we are meeting is locked. (Palestinian time runs, how do I say this? with less urgency? perhaps related to the cycles of the moon? Still trying to figure this out as an obsessive Westerner.) He is talking about how the Palestinian Authority is "existentially necessary" for Israel, how a single democratic state is the long-term goal, not ideal but a more ethical solution than anything else.

We get ushered into an open office and Omar starts officially talking; words just pour out of him so rapidly, succinctly; I struggle to keep up. Things have really changed in the past year. What many do not realize is that BDS is now a mainstream Palestinian movement that is supported by almost everyone, it is not an isolated fringe activity. Even Fatah supports BDS. The strategy is anchored in international law and, Omar explains, "Targets Israel because it is a regime of occupation and apartheid. This is not about being Jewish." The Israeli establishment clearly considers BDS a strategic threat. Netanyahu mentioned BDS eighteen times when he gave his talk to the UN; second only to Iran (but who's counting?). Omar states, "Israel does not know what to do with nonviolent movements." This defeats the narrative of the Palestinian as terrorist. I think of the Israeli official who admitted, "We do not do Gandhi well."

While there are well funded, well organized efforts to Brand Israel as a "beacon of democracy" (to quote Netanyahu), to highlight Israeli artists, academics, gays, to present a "pretty face," "all this washing [i.e., pink washing, green washing, etc.] gets wiped out by one massacre."

In 2014, Omar asserts BDS is in a different place: the financial, economic sphere. The Gates Foundation recently divested from G4S, a private security company which is known to torture prisoners, builds the Israeli security apparatus, and is deeply involved in the occupation. The CEO of G4S committed not to renew the contract with Israeli prisons, the first time such a public statement has been made. It does not matter that BDS was not mentioned. It does matter that a large company decides that it is too (economically? politically? strategically?) costly to do business with the Israeli state. Obviously, pressure will continue until the company comes through on its promise.

Omar informs us that major banks and pension funds in Europe have divested from the top five Israeli banks involved in the occupied territories. Apparently the Dutch are saying that if these banks have operations with companies in the territories, they will divest from the entire bank. "Do not punish the crime, punish the criminal."

It has always been difficult to figure out which products come from the settlements, and Omar agrees that it is too hard to boycott settlement products. They are often disguised or relabeled (like from the Netherlands), but it is very realistic to boycott companies that operate in the occupied territories, so the tactic should be boycotting companies rather than products. I take note of this development.

Unlike my Massachusetts governor, who is swooning over high tech ventures with Israeli companies, the German government announced that it will not work with all high tech Israeli companies including those in East Jerusalem. The European Union is not joining the BDS movement but implementing their own guidelines in response to grassroots pressure, so they will not give grants for research in the territories. The Luxemburg pension fund divested from the top five Israeli banks. The Norwegian pension fund divested from Israeli companies involved in settlements, but then they took Africa Israel off the list because the company denied involvement. The Israeli group Who Profits? went to the Jewish settlement of Gilo and documented their presence, but Africa Israel said that Gilo is not in the occupied territories (you know, just part of the expanding Jerusalem neighborhoods). Organizers demanded that they consult the United Nations, who might know a bit more about international law, and the Norwegians got the message and divested. From 2013–14, four US academic organizations endorsed BDS. These are all major developments. Really big.

Omar has a subtle kind of sarcasm. He says that the Israeli government has been totally hijacked by the settler movement and this is new. The labor party is a kind of "smarter Zionism," but the leadership is now a "dumber Zionism." Israel is no longer even pretending to stand for peace, coexistence, etc. The academic and cultural boycotts have tarnished the Israeli brand. Even John Kerry acknowledged that there was something seriously wrong with settlement building. In much of Europe, people choose not to buy Israeli products. "We rely on the grassroots to build pressure," even though in the international world, "the Israeli government is untouchable," is not held accountable for obvious unjust practices. So, "do one church, one university at a time."

The delegates want to talk about the nitty gritty, on-the-ground issues that come up. Omar is asked if there are any mutual funds that are BDS compliant. "Not yet, but it is in process." He explains that SRIs (socially responsible investing) do not use BDS language (though they traditionally avoid military and environmentally damaging companies), but the change is coming.

We then engage in a fascinating discussion that speaks to Jewish privilege and Jewish power on the left. At the Jewish Voice for Peace conference last year, Omar spoke. He notes that support-ive Jewish voices on the BDS issue give it legitimacy and fend off the accusation of anti-Semitism. At the same time, Jewish voices run the risk of expropriating Palestinian voices, thus entrenching Jewish exceptionalism and maintaining the belief that only Jews are "allowed" to criticize Israeli policy. This actually is a form of anti-Semitism, a promotion of the fear of Jews; of powerful Jews who will destroy you if you criticize Israel (thus you need the cover of left-wing Jews). This is not good for anyone, but many Zionist groups thrive on this fear.

Omar maintains that while Jewish voices are critical, it is equally critical to work in coalition, such as with the American Friends Service Committee, the Presbyterians, Adalah New York, etc. Jewish Voice for Peace, who initiated the TIAA-CREF divestment campaign, pressuring the company to divest from companies that profit from occupation in their SRI portfolio, now works in a wider coalition called WE DIVEST; they are careful not to monopolize the movement but are ready to counter the charge of anti-Semitism. The recent success in Boston with ending a Veolia contract is related to a large coalition that included union groups as well as Jewish and other faith-based organizations who brought a wide variety of complaints against the company, one of which included its behavior in the occupied territories.

Another delegate wonders how to work in academic institutions like Brandeis University that are largely hostile to the BDS movement where there are something like eight "pro-Israel groups," (I would like to redefine what it means to be pro-Israel, but that is for another conversation.) Omar explains that he went to Columbia University in the 1980s, where there were twenty "pro-Israel" groups from right to left, and six "pro-Palestinian students." They felt completely isolated, so they found coalitions with Blacks, Latinos, feminists, and liberal Zionists who were opposed to the occupation (which was a radical idea back then). They worked on mutual interests such as opposing war, improving the environment. He reminds us that now as well as then, it is important to select a target that makes sense within your community, look for levels of complicity in international law for instance, and potential for cross-movement work; the company's offenses have to go beyond oppressing Palestinians. Thus it makes no sense to go after a company that makes some great cancer drug in Israel or the settlements, but it makes a lot of sense to link the activities of G4S in building the US-Mexico wall and walls in the territories. "Trying and failing is not okay unless it leads to education, otherwise it is not strategic."

But what if there are no Palestinian-led BDS organizations, like in Boston, where there is a lot of BDS activity? Omar advises that we must fill the vacuum until the Palestinian community becomes more active. There are lots of challenges that discourage Palestinians in the United States, from fears related to targeting post-9/11 to Islamophobia. Omar remarks that many in that community are not politically active, but their sons and daughters are. He notes that campus based Students for Justice in Palestine (SJPs) are no longer having Jewish leadership and that leadership is often coming from Palestinian women. "I understand having Palestinian voices up front, but this is a universal issue. I do not believe in identity politics. The anti-apartheid movement was my movement. I was doing something right as a human, I own this as my own struggle." Focus on effectiveness, the quality of the work, anti-racist principles.

In response to another question about how to work in progressive community organizations that partner with Israeli groups on community development, racial and economic justice issues, etc., Omar suggests that we need to broaden the conversation, to "South Africanize the issue." As an example he asks, what would we have done if Boston University was working with a South African university on cancer treatment during the apartheid era? Yes, that is good for humanity, but the research institution is also complicit within an apartheid system, and this collaboration would have been inappropriate. He suggests we ask Palestinians about joint research projects with, for instance, Tel Aviv University. It is fine to do research with Israelis but not with Israeli funding (i.e., institutions). So, in our hypothetical case, Boston University should fund the research not Tel Aviv University, thus not legitimizing a university that is complicit in the occupation. In the same vein, Israeli filmmakers, artists, and poets can be invited to festivals in a "BDS friendly way." For instance, at the Edinburgh festival, the Israeli embassy in London paid a filmmaker to screen her film. The festival was told that if they accepted this money, people would boycott the festival. The festival returned the money from the Israeli filmmaker and paid for her to show the Israeli film; "there must be no institutional links." In another example, Omar explains that a Canadian LGBT artist in a Scottish festival found out that an Israeli artist was sponsored by the Israeli foreign ministry. The Canadian put pressure on the festival, wrote a letter to every artist. The Israeli embassy said the artist is pro-Palestinian, this is a dissenting voice, etc. "But we do not care about content; this is not about censorship, it is about funding." The Israeli sponsorship was cancelled and the artist came to the festival.

A particular challenge involves communities of color, who often come to Israel on religious pilgrimages or as cultural exchanges. Omar explains, "It is easy to get a free trip to Israel, so South Africanize the issue." If you want to come on a "fact finding mission, then do it without complicity, do not cross the picket line. This is happening more and more. Israel helps us to convert people, if they come on an honest fact finding mission, they see what is going on." We talk about our African American governor, Deval Patrick, as a particularly challenging case. Omar advises that the "the black community is key to BDS, we need to win them." There is already a high conversion rate among young Jews (see the work of Peter Beinart), who at this point are largely somewhere between apathetic about Israel to supportive of Palestinian rights, but clearly different than their Zionist parents and grandparents. The Israel machine focuses on African Americans, Native Americans, the Asian community, framing the issue as, "Jews are the indigenous people!" "Join us in our struggle." Colonialism is conveniently overlooked. African Americans, students, women leaders, are invited to Israel to promote an historic Jewish–Black alliance, we led the civil rights movement and we can do it again.

Friends of Sabeel, the Kairos document, and Christian liberation theology work to counter this Zionist ideology, but it is a frustratingly slow process. Omar advises us that, thinking of the recent alliance between Cornell University and the Technion, the Israeli establishment will continue to score big successes at high levels; the US establishment is profoundly "pro-Israel," (in the classic use of that word). "Forget the big elephants, chip away, and attack smaller things. The Technion was not selected because it was the best, there was a well-planned conspiracy and work was done before to make it happen."

I am beginning to feel like a white civil rights activist working in the Deep South in the 1960s. The parallels are striking and the historical connection revives me. Time to take all of this conversation home.

Water and Salt

We meet with Randa Wahbe, the dedicated and articulate advocacy officer at Addameer, on the sixty-first day of the longest hunger strike by administrative detainees in Israeli jails. The strike is a political strike, i.e., not for improved prison conditions but for ending the Israeli policy of detaining people without charges or adequate access to a lawyer, sometimes for years; six years or more is not uncommon. At the time of our meeting, there had been no negotiations, but as I write this a week later, the strike has ended, some secret deal has been met, and there is mostly speculation: What was decided? Did the hunger strikers feel that this was not the right time when the public is obsessed by the three missing settlers and the World Cup and Ramadan? Who knows?

Whatever the outcome, prisoner issues are central to Palestinian liberation; eight hundred thousand Palestinians have been arrested since 1967, 40% of the male population. Thousands of Palestinians are held in this limbo land of administrative detention. The striking prisoners are put into isolation, cannot go outside or have family visits (they often do not see their families because of permitting and travel issues anyway). The prisoners receive monetary fines taken from their canteen account. Sometimes they have limited or no access to lawyers or they are transferred around to different prison hospitals so the lawyer cannot locate them. At the time of our visit, there were at least 130 hunger strikers, the movement was growing and may have reached 300. The hunger strikers are beaten, denied medical care, and are only treated by prison doctors (who clearly have lost their ethical compass), who are known to be abusive, dangle food or force-feeding tubes in their faces. Prisoners are shackled twelve hours per day and, as you can imagine, the conditions are pretty horrific.

The prisoners were drinking water and salt for fourteen days; Randa reports the Israeli authorities then denied them salt, some may be taking some unknown supplements that "barely keep them alive. As an organization, we are very concerned because of the lack of negotiation between the Israeli prison service and the prisoners, will there by martyrs?" A lot of administrative detainees are older than sixty and not striking, but other prisoners are striking in sympathy. There appears to be a trend to arrest Palestinians shortly after their eighteenth birthday as they can be tried as adults. The youngest hunger striker was arrested five days after his eighteenth birthday, "He is still a child, but he has been in prison for two years." There have been over four hundred arrests since the 12th of June; seventy-seven are in administrative detention.

And then there is the heart-breaking issue of child arrests. Although Israel technically changed its policy and has child courts, Randa reports that children are treated like adults. They are often arrested between midnight and five a.m., families don't know where they are going. They are interrogated without a lawyer, not allowed to see their families. The military court judge is the same as for adults and Randa explains that the children are routinely tortured by their interrogators. This is mostly psychological torture, threats that they will be killed, sexual abuse; they are put into solitary confinement, have florescent lights on twenty-four hours per day, are placed in stress positions, and beaten. The forced confessions are then used to arrest adults in the community. So imagine you are an eighteen-year-old boy, you have seen your father and grandfather humiliated at checkpoints, you have watched settlers steal your land and water, and, very possibly, you have thrown stones at a passing Israeli jeep that has arrived to make your life a living hell. And then you crack in prison and are responsible for your own brother's arrest. Many children never return to school, develop bed-wetting and behavioral problems. With these brutal policies, we are witnessing the slow destruction of Palestinian society and the creation of environments that will create more angry, hopeless, militant men seeking revenge. In Silwan, there is a fourteen-year-old who has been arrested six times, mostly for throwing stones, according to IDF soldiers or settlers. So why are we doing this Mr. Netanyahu? Palestinian parents pay fines to release their children, and last year, Palestinians paid thirteen million shekels into the Israeli military court, in a bizarre sense, financing their own imprisonment. And did I mention that prisons are increasingly privatized, sort of like the United States?

In general, Randa explains, administrative detention under international law is allowed if an individual is threatening the security of the state. This should be used rarely. But in Israel, the military claims the Shin Bet has "secret files" that show that this person is a threat to the state. "This is used arbitrarily, there are obviously no files. Let's look at who gets arrested: prominent activists, academics, regular folks. Recently a political scientist was released, after two-and-a-half years without any charges. He has no idea why he was arrested this time, [suffice it to say that] he is an academic who writes about resistance, attends demonstrations, and has been in and out of prison for years. One of the hunger strikers is a prominent community member, part of an agricultural union who promotes farmers' rights; he has been in and out of administrative detention for years and was rearrested in February."

At the time of our visit, a bill to allow forced feeding was to be voted on in the Israeli Knesset, although forced feeding is regarded as a form of torture, people have died during the procedure, and it is used to break the strikers. Even the Israeli Medical Association is against it. The bill did not pass, but today (June 30, 2014) the Knesset is voting on another bill that would permit doctors to do forced feeding without risk of punishment. Netanyahu has framed this as an issue of internal security: forced feeding is for the safety of Israeli citizens, because if a prisoner dies, "it will threaten security of Israelis in Judea and Samaria." And then they play with words, artificial (not forced) feeding, moderate restraints (rather than the full shackling that is used), etc., etc. The doctor has to recommend forced feeding, "for the benefit of the prisoner"; this is signed off by a district court, which gives the whole process the air of legality.

In the last month, there have been other worrisome bills: one to deny amnesty to prisoners who are released in exchanges (Israel has released seventy prisoners arrested before Oslo in 1993); this perpetuates the definition of prisoner as automatic permanent terrorist. Pro-prisoner demonstrations were suppressed by the Palestinian Authority and the IDF, especially in Hebron, where there was a demonstration by mothers of prisoners. Since June 12, five Palestinians have been killed, and, in addition to the four hundred arrested, there have been eight hundred home incursions, lots of injuries and road closures. The Palestinian Authority has security coordination with Israel, which is facilitating the siege on Hebron. Two nights ago in Ramallah, PA officers shot demonstrators storming the police station. Currently this is the largest military operation since the Second Intifada, and for me, the strangeness is that it is largely happening under cover of darkness. By the time the sun comes up, most of the Israeli forces are out of the villages and homes and universities and everything looks deceptively normal unless you live in Hebron. The world community may not even notice, there are no tanks and no phosphorus bombs to catch anyone's attention.

Randa talks about a host of other human rights concerns and the picture is grim. Children born to mothers in prison are kept in prison for two years with no extra space, food, or medical care; they are basically born with a prison record. Pregnant Palestinian women who are arrested get no prenatal care, no special food, etc., and give birth shackled. The prisons are dirty, prisoners have to purchase their needs from a canteen, there are often no family visits; it is an utterly dehumanizing climate. There is a case now that won't allow a granddaughter to visit her grandfather, the courts say they have to prove their relation to each other, or mothers are asked to prove their relationship to their children in prison.

When people are released, there is some support from the ministry of prisoner affairs, dedicated to legal aid, financial and medical assistance, but not many resources available for rehabilitation. The prison experience is so normalized within the community, there is lots of community support, but not much treatment for PTSD (posttraumatic stress disorder), which just about everyone has. Interestingly, there is no housing or employment discrimination; the community views these as largely political arrests.

If arrested, there is a higher rate of rearrest, the IDF targets former prisoners, which basically destroys their lives. There are students who have been attending Birzeit University for eight years because they are repeatedly arrested around exam times, and their education just drags on, or students arrested during the final year of high school so they cannot take the exams critical for university admission.

So why do people get arrested? For starters, there are sixteen hundred military orders that govern life under occupation. (Yes Virginia, there is an occupation; the place is not administered or liberated or whatever euphemism you may hear.) Organizations like student unions and all political organizations are illegal, including technically the Palestinian Authority. This gives the IDF very broad discretionary powers. People get arrested because they are activists like those in Stop the Wall or because they do volunteer work to empower youth. Basically the charges are used to suppress Palestinian resistance in all forms. Randa notes that there have been three arrests of Addameer colleagues in the past year, charged with giving legal advice to youth about interrogation, which is after all part of their job description. "We are all in jeopardy… Going to a demonstration today we could be charged, this is the climate."

Randa was studying at a university in the United States and was involved in their Students for Justice in Palestine. She moved to Jordan to learn Arabic, came for a conference; Addameer had an opening and she took the job. While her family is still in California (and it is often hard for Palestinians to get a visa), she believes that it is important for Diaspora Palestinians to come back and to do the challenging work of ending the occupation and its immense hardships.

You can read the Addameer website for further depressing details about the realities of military occupation. Think about how Palestinians are portrayed in our media (the boy with the sling shot, why exactly is he throwing that rock and why not portray university students arrested during exams? Doesn't fit the stereotype?) Think about the meaning of resistance and the unchecked power of an occupying force. And the next time you pay your taxes, think about our US military industrial complex that provides the weaponry and machinery that makes this military power possible.

Building Dreamers in a Nightmare

I write this blog belatedly about a visit to the Old City of Jerusalem and Yasser Qous, an Afro-Palestinian who runs a youth center in a cavernous stone structure dating back to the twelfth century. And because this is about two visits in June that now feel like a decade ago, I need to acknowledge the murder of the three Hebron settler youth and the frightening revenge/pogrom- like behavior that now characterizes the Israeli military and some of its citizens. Perhaps if you get to know some of the folks who are now at risk (i.e., any Palestinian), although they were at risk before, it was just more invisible, you too will be filled with dread and worry and horror.

Yasser Qous is wearing a dashiki and has a warm, open face, a shaved head, and a rolled cigarette in his mouth. He is dark, has very expressive hands, and an intelligent, laid back manner. He says, "The Old City is like our house," and welcomes us as if we are his personal guests. He grew up here, became active as a student at Bethlehem University, his father came from Chad in 1952. He works with city youth doing photography and alternative media, and he is involved in psychosocial interventions around issues like drugs and sexual abuse. He comments that there are no addiction treatment centers, that drug use is a symptom of hopelessness and lack of opportunity, and thus it is a political problem. His program is preventive rather than treatment-oriented. He finds that the Israeli government is only concerned with drug use when it starts affecting Jewish youth. There are the usual stories of house demolitions and a new policy of house arrest for teens.

We see a drop-in café with sprawling couches, drinks, and ice cream, and a TV that is nonstop World Cup. He is very excited about the upcoming Ramadan events; there is a competition between neighborhoods for the best light decorations. (The Old City is starting to look a bit like Christmas in Queens.) He explains that the rituals of Ramadan include all night celebrations with Sufi dancing and music, followed by quiet (thirsty) days. I am told that hunger is less of an issue around day three of the fast, which lasts from the morning prayer (three to four-ish a.m.) until sunset (in the unforgiving Mediterranean heat).

Since unemployment is such a huge problem in East Jerusalem (60% poverty rate for Palestinians in East Jerusalem), the center is involved in training and supporting small business. They are part of a tourism coalition that sells handicrafts, but the crafts are all from Nablus and Hebron. "What is the East Jerusalem identity?" he asks. The center is involved in reviving East Jerusalem handicrafts based on research and training. They have a good relationship with a French development agency and an upcoming project involves supporting ten street sellers (they all need permission from Israel). Twenty youth will be trained to create a photo studio on Al-Wad Street (the main street); they will take photos of the Old City and sell them, create and sell handmade accessories, and do alternative, socially oriented tours from four p.m. to midnight. They also do art and music, have a band, dance *dabke* (traditional Palestinian dance), hip-hop, and Brazilian *capoeira*. They have made good relationships with African American students from the United States and did an event for a South African representative.

Yasser explains that most Africans came in the fifteenth century to Jerusalem as Muslim pilgrims on the hajj (to pray at Mecca and Al Aqsa), but many settled here, particularly towards the end of the Ottoman Empire and during the British Mandate when it became more difficult to go home. This youth center was previously a prison after the Arab revolt, before that a compound/hospice called a *ribat* [see Wikipedia: "a ribat (Arabic: رباط) ribāt, hospice, hostel, base or retreat... These fortifications later served to protect commercial routes, and as centers for isolated Muslim communities. Ribats were first seen in the 8th century."]. This compound is the oldest *ribat* in Jerusalem, founded by a Mamluk sultan who brought slaves from Egypt.

With the British Mandate, the property went to the Mufti and the African community settled here. After 1948, half left to Jordan, some to Lebanon, and others to Jericho, Tulkarem, Khan Younis in Gaza, and the Negev. There are now 350 mostly Afro-Palestinians in Jerusalem out of a total 183,000 Palestinians in the East Jerusalem municipality; they call themselves "coconuts," Black outside, Palestinian inside. Their main connection with each other lies with the hajj. They have been part of Palestinian resistance, martyrs in all the wars, and many have been imprisoned. The first female political prisoner was Afro-Palestinian and she spent thirteen years incarcerated. The neighborhood is subjected to frequent collective punishment at the hands of Israeli security. Many have intermarried with Palestinians; "marriage is between families, not individuals; we want someone from the same class." They are proud of their roots but not well-connected to Africa, are Muslims and Christians, and face discrimination (Black, Palestinian, lower class) and high unemployment in Jerusalem. Most are from Nigeria, Senegal, Sudan, and Chad.

A week later, he takes the delegation on a tour of East Jerusalem, through the many Muslim and Christian sites. Warning: I find religion very problematic here. We are talking the BIG ONES like the Fourteen Stations of the Cross and the Church of the Holy Sepulcher—where Christ was crucified, for the Jews and atheists and generally uninformed in the group. We are swarmed with teeming Christians of all colors and stripes, each tour in different colored tee shirts or hats; they are obviously deeply moved by the religious holiness experience that seeps in everywhere in this ancient, complicated city. Interesting tidbit: by legal tradition, a Muslim family opens and closes the Church of the Holy Sepulcher each day because there was too much fighting for the honor between the many Christian sects. (Sigh, Christian values?) He keeps advising us to "stay in the shadow" so we won't get roasted by the sun. A right-wing Jewish group, Ateret Cohanim, which conveniently has established a yeshiva in the Muslim Quarter, using Palestinian collaborators, rents and sells houses to Jews and displaces Palestinians. (Jewish values? Oops, displacement is the goal). We see four Jewish families in their gated and guarded home, armed guards walk the Jews out of the Muslim Quarter to the Jewish Quarter (which was depopulated of Jews in 1948 when it was taken by the Jordanians). Yasser explains that not only are these folks expanding into Muslim and Christian sectors (no one else can get permits FYI), but they are creating a Jewish ghetto for themselves. In the Jewish sector, which is obviously well-funded and pristine from an archeological and touristic point of view, along with the arty shops, great jewelry, etc., there is evidence of all the different conquerors who built on top of the preexisting civilizations lo these many centuries. We wander down the Cardo, the ancient Roman market with a multistory excavation that goes deep into the ground. Armed security guards escort herds of young children to their destinations, and I can only think they look like tough teen boy babysitters with guns and walkie talkies and what are the children learning from this daily experience? Life is dangerous and "they" all want to kill us? The abnormal becomes normalized.

The youth center created the Longest Chain of Readers at Damascus Gate, six thousand kids reading books and then donating them to libraries. They were celebrating a kite festival with three hundred children, but the Israeli Defense Forces attacked the event and destroyed the kites. (Do they really have to be this way?)

When Yasser was ten years old he was given a book, *Children of Palestine*, and the introduction explained that life is like theater, there is the audience and there are the players. It was at that point he decided that he wanted to be a player. Just imagine the dreams that were crushed in those flying kites. So why are kids throwing stones? Wouldn't you?

June 24, 2014

Travelling while Occupied

Blogging retrospectively is a challenge, I am reporting from the ground and the ground is in constant seismic shift mode.

Let me acknowledge that the deaths of the three kidnapped Israeli youths, Gilad Shaer, Naftali Fraenkel, and Eyal Yifrach, provided the Israeli leadership with the opportunity to unleash a horrific barrage of military might, home incursions, arrests, and killings that had little to do with a careful investigation of the crime and the capture of the perpetrators. Collective punishment is still all the rage, and at this point I would just call it official policy. Even the Israeli generals are trying to tone down the "let's destroy Hamas" rhetoric coming out of our dear prime minister's mouth. The abduction, killing, and burning of Mohammed Abu Khdeir, on the other hand, is being approached in a totally different manner; there is the police statement that they are not sure if the murder was "nationalistic," i.e., done by an Israeli, or "criminal," i.e., done by a Palestinian. Then there was the false rumor put out by the police that Mohammed was gay and that this was some kind of revenge killing by the homophobic family (not). To the Palestinians in Shuafat, a neighborhood of East Jerusalem, this is clearly a revenge killing, and to my eye, given the explosion of Arab hatred, the attempt two days earlier to kidnap a ten-year-old called Mousa Zalum (his parents called the police, no one responded), and the gangs of right-wing Jewish teenagers roaming the streets of Jerusalem chanting "Death to the Arabs!" I vote with the Palestinians. Maybe we should just go demolish a few Israeli homes and arrest a bunch of teenagers, probably start with the lovelies in Hebron and Kiryat Arba; oh, but we don't do that to Jews. As East Jerusalem explodes, the police use live fire on the inhabitants in the neighborhood (East Jerusalem ID carriers and Israeli citizens, also read: not Jews).

To give this a little context, according to official statistics, since September 2000, more than fourteen hundred Palestinian children have been killed by the Israeli military, which is equivalent to one child killed every three days, and some six thousand injured in the past thirteen or so years. I think a year of national mourning is in order, but this is a military occupation and well, what can I say about who counts and who doesn't. Which brings us to some other realities of daily life.

I was hoping to tell you more about the realities of occupation, in particular, travelling while occupied. I (and every Palestinian I know) dreads Qalandia checkpoint, the major checkpoint between Jerusalem and Ramallah. It is a chaotic, traffic-plagued military terminal with guard towers and concrete walls and grimy garbage and narrow turnstiles, and people waiting, waiting, waiting. Faces range from utter resignation and defeat to outright indignation and rage. I vary.

There is a sign on entry that says in English and Arabic: "Please keep terminal clean," but the Hebrew reads: "Please keep order and cleanliness." Can't trust those frisky Arabs to stay in line. People queue in narrow chutes, two to three feet wide, with vertical, floor-to-ceiling bars and an excruciatingly narrow turnstile that makes passage with luggage, shopping bags, or small children a humiliating joke. The turnstile is controlled by the Israeli security and I note that even the green light does not necessarily mean the bars will turn. Once in the maze, bags are x-rayed and I walk through the metal detector. Sometimes in protest I do not take off my watch and the metal detector buzzes and no one cares, sometimes they do. I then approach a bulletproof window where I press my passport up against the glass and sometimes get the attention of a twenty-something in uniform on the other side. Sometimes not. There is always a cup of coffee or a phone call or… Communication is challenging. Two members of our delegation were pulled aside for extra security investigation and were asked questions like: "Do you love Israel?" "Are you afraid of us?" "Are you sure you are not an Israeli citizen?" "Do you love Palestinians?" (Really). Then there are more turnstiles of the humiliation you-are-a-rat-in-a-cage and-we-really-control-you-in-case-you-did-not-already-get-the-message variety and then you are free to fight for a taxi or a bus or a *service* with the license plate appropriate for whichever side you are on now. On the "other side" I note a sign in Arabic that says "Judea and Samaria," in case you are not clear on the concept. My recollection is that there is a sign in English that says, "Have a good day!" or some such thing.

So I was thinking, if I were bent on revenge or strapped in a suicide vest (this is all about security right?) would I really hazard a visit through Qalandia? I think not. So what is this massive, time-consuming, demoralizing daily exercise about? Control and humiliation comes to mind. Also, it might just be easier to stay home and skip that visit to Al Aqsa this year, if one were lucky enough to get a permit in the first place.

June 25, 2014

Teaching in the Ghetto

The Jerusalem neighborhood of Abu Dis ended up on the wrong side of the wall. Every time bus #36 from East Jerusalem turns this particular corner, there is the monstrous "barrier" (which is quite a euphemism), up close and personal, all eight meters high of poured concrete stretching along the edge of the road (or rather defining the edge of the road and in some ways, the edge of existence); I have the distinct impression that military-city planner types are giving us and all the wrong-side-people, a gigantic concrete finger in the eye. Most of Al Quds University is on the wrong side too if you live in Jerusalem, and of course on the right side if you live in Ramallah or Tulkarem or Jenin or Hebron. For students who are old enough to remember, getting to school from East Jerusalem used to be easy and quick. Now, the journey involves a long tunnel, skirting Ma'ale Adumim (one of the largest Jewish settlements or shall we just be honest and say colonies on the West Bank), swinging through Bethany (the biblical one which seems more industrial, and auto shops and less Jesus, Lazarus, and lepers), and making a huge snaking swing east and south to get to the bedraggled neighborhood of Abu Dis. Let's not even mention the increased use of fuel, the challenged shock absorbers that need constant repair, the choking air pollution, the lost time and rising aggravation, and the need to plan life around buses and permits and when is it safe in the first place to try the daring trip to school. What do these people have to complain about anyway????

We meet with Hani Abdeen, the dignified and somewhat burned out dean of the medical school, neat mustache, wire rimmed glasses, striped shirt, very old school, and I feel like this should be called "soldiering on against all odds." Al Quds Medical School was founded in 1994 and graduated its fourteenth class last week, for a total of 720 graduates to date. Hani is very pleased with his students. He brags that they do very well on qualifying exams for residencies all over the Western world: Canada, United States, Europe. "The students are doing a good job, under duress people excel. We do not have a large faculty, all the resources, teaching materials, yet with all these shortcomings students do well. In the USMLE (US Medical Licensing Exam) Palestinian students are in the top 1% of foreign graduates." What doesn't kill you makes you stronger.

This is of particular interest to me as the health and human rights project was involved in starting an exchange program between Harvard and Al Quds Medical School and the students rotate through Harvard hospitals and receive "glowing reports." Hani is very worried that while the medical school is doing a good job, they are essentially "training doctors for America, there is a big brain drain. Once they see how good life is, the standards of medicine, they leave and stay where they train." He notes this is a problem for all of the third world.

Sadly, "even if they train, but should come back, we are starved of medical personnel." Hani notes that there is not one well-trained hematologist or nephrologist in the occupied territories, and this is true in much of surgery, medicine, and ob-gyn as well. I am surprised to hear him say, "One way to address this: how to change ratio male to female. He notes that now the medical school class is 60% female and he wants to increase this to 75% females, "because they stay, they are more loyal to their societies, stay with families and are more of use to the Palestinian popula-tion!" His theory is that females, "do much better on post high school exams, have less diversions, are more focused, while males have other goals, politics, etc." He wonders if women, "may be more intelligent, or more driven to try to prove themselves." I am not sure how to wrap my brain around this reverse sexism, but I have to agree, this is a creative solution to a vexing problem. I secretly wonder if once again, women hold up (more than) half the sky, put up with the less dynamic careers, and keep the family functional.

"We don't have good residency training, do not have the hospi-tals, and Israelis do not let us. Everything you build, then there is a fracas and then the whole thing collapses again. This is a big prob-lem. Two days ago, the IDF entered the university at night, wreaked havoc on the infrastructure," and they did the same at a university in Jenin and another in Bethlehem (remember the policy of collective punishment). There are repeated mass arrests of students and professors (collective punishment—still illegal under international law). "Obviously what is happening, the Israelis are not interested in Palestinians having their own entity, all they want is ethnic cleansing, get rid of Palestinians and evict them. We are trying to develop, but nipped in the bud... We are fed up with all this talk about human rights. This is how it is on the ground... It makes your blood boil, there is a limit; what are the Israelis trying to do? They have Nobel laureates, etc., in Israel, but don't they understand what is going on?"

The grinding reality is revealed by the fact that three weeks ago students were about to start two weeks of final exams. But students from Hebron (twenty-five of eighty) couldn't get permits, so the exams were delayed, and now as the clampdown continues (people with IDs from Hebron are unable to travel), students are taking their exams at home from a computer or on pen and paper (you know, that little problem of needing electricity and internet connection while occupied), so the work is multiplied.

"Imagine [a student] prepared for exam, then cannot take it, then [the exams are] bunched together, this creates psychological trauma, [but] we do not have enough psychiatrists. There is not one child psychiatrist in the occupied territories." Students get supports from tutors, secretaries. "One of our faculty's house was ransacked in the night, I do not know why." He lived in Hebron, guilty as charged. "This happened to students' families as well, imagine preparing for exams, the students seventeen to eighteen years old," and then the "oasis of democracy in Mideast" enters their bedrooms at night, finger on the trigger. So what does a seventeen-year-old do with all that trauma and rage?

Hani describes what is going on, "It is madness. We need to educate Israeli society, the majority is ignorant of what is happening in the West Bank. The separation wall is a psychological barrier. They have succeeded, everyone behind the wall is a terrorist, and they are not interested in knowing what is happening. What is needed, to educate Israelis, how to get out of their isolation ghetto mentality. We are also in a ghetto, two ghettos, this is more important than educating the Arab world. Human life is sacred, if you want to live with neighbors peacefully, then why are you doing this… Arabs, what have they done to Israelis? How many [Israelis] killed in buses? They [IDF] killed over one thousand people in Gaza. This is disproportionate killings; they are all the same, even doctors are participating in force feeding prisoners."

Hani's exasperated frustration is palpable. He states he is, "disenchanted with building bridges, when it comes to the crunch, they are professional killers. It is heartbreaking as a medical professional, those people who they are detaining have not participated in any crimes." There is "no court of law."

We try to focus on the medical school, a six-year program that starts after high school. Hani describes a traditional curriculum that is changing to a more integrated, organ-based approach next year. The first three years involve basic sciences, the last three years are clinical. They are also planning on a graduate entry program, four years of medical training after college, like most US programs. Students at Al Quds do their clinical rotations at affiliated hospitals like Al Mokassed, Augusta Victoria, St. Johns, and the Red Crescent Hospital in Jerusalem and hospitals in Hebron, Ramallah, and Jericho in the West Bank. He says there is a curriculum for the different clinical settings, but this is in theory only. The hitch is that the first-rate hospitals are all in East Jerusalem, so only the students who can get permits to enter Jerusalem can go on these rotations, and the rest of the students are forced to train in what are seen as second-rate facilities.

But medical care is even more complicated. The Ministry of Health runs community-based clinics, and the NGO Palestinian Medical Relief Society has clinics that are focused on providing health care to poorly served communities. Hani suggests that all of these settings have issues around quality of care and he wants his students to learn medicine, "in a proper manner." The quality issue is a big one. There are "no post graduate courses here," no continuing medical education courses (in the United States, I am required to do fifty hours of CMEs per year and that is part of the task of staying up-to-date). Additionally, "Everyone doesn't have a computer, cannot travel, cannot access villages, so logistics are a big problem." The school has no connection with UNRWA, the UN agency that provides health care in the refugee camps, and that care tends to be low quality, overwhelmed, and underfunded.

In Gaza, the medical school Al Azhar is under the tutelage of Al Quds, and the Hamas-run Islamic University also has the same curriculum. Yes, there are medical students filled with aspirations and drive in Gaza and they get caught in the incursions and the phosphorus bombs along with everyone else. Hani reports that the graduates do well despite the conditions, although the last time I checked, the Gaza hospitals were still recovering from being bombed to smithereens and unable to rebuild basic infrastructure like drinkable water and stocked pharmacies, so I suspect he is being a bit upbeat here. There is also a medical school in Nablus, called An-Najah.

Hani notes that the French government offers scholarships to two to three postgraduate students a year for PhDs in medical science or specialty training, others go to Jordan or the United Kingdom, "but they never come back." He explains that the students make commitments to return, but then they buy themselves out. They are the top 1% in Palestine, high achievers, they want to be good doctors, but "our hospitals and infrastructure are not conducive to that. Nursing is not that good, physical therapy is not that good. It is not a solid team, so it is much harder to do medicine here. The pay is better, standard of living, career development all better outside."

I wonder why Hani is still here. He trained in the United Kingdom, but "my mother was ill and alone so I came back [thinking] I will stay for a year and then I got myself sucked up." The immense need, the possibility to build something better, the inertia and grinding difficulty of getting through each day let alone planning a career or an escape, the small victories and sense of place, and then family and commitment, and decades later… he finds himself still here, talking politics and medicine with some curious folks from the United States who are trying to understand.

Medicine: If It Doesn't Kill You, It Makes You Strong

The meeting with the medical students is not that polite. Now I will grant you they had just finished their exams (because of the Hebron curfew and the resultant delays, some had six exams in one day). Many are about to graduate, so they are so done with all the frustrations and they are living in a variety of ghettos trying to get an education in an impossible place (and FYI, my recollection of medical school is also filled with anger and frustration and I did not cross one checkpoint). They have a lot to say and are obviously happy that there are some curious people interested in listening. One student describes Al Quds as "six years of hell." The students from East Jerusalem discuss the frustrations of crossing the Qalandia checkpoint twice a day, most everyone has had some frightening experience with a gun-toting Israeli who is also their age and sees every Palestinian as a terrorist, everyone complains about the uptight culture of medicine (sounds a lot like the hierarchical culture of hospitals in the 1970s), physicians who act "like gods," and of course, there are longstanding conflicts with the administration.

As we try to tease apart the miseries of medical school in general from the miseries of this medical school in this place in particular, certain themes emerge. Al Quds (as opposed to An-Najah in Nablus) has no teaching hospital, so students get dispersed all over. Students with IDs or permits for East Jerusalem get better clinical rotations and there are no standards or clear-cut expectations in the clinical curriculum, so the teaching is enormously variable and sometimes totally inadequate. (Pediatrics at Al Mokassed hospital is a glowing exception.) The doctors are often brilliant, have trained in high power institutions abroad, but are very busy, have active private clinics, and teaching medical students is often low on their list of priorities. In addition, unlike hospitals in the United States, residents (where they exist) are not required to teach the students, so "everything is personal connection."

The students would love to see the institution improve and are aware that Al Quds has funding issues, that the Israeli authorities are not allowing them to build a teaching hospital in Jerusalem. It

There are many professional looking types, men and women, and two rows of guys in army green and berets, apparently soldiers from the Palestinian Authority also have a lot to learn about torture (i.e., why they shouldn't do it), prevention, and treatment. On the stage, I recognize Dr. Mustafa Barghouti, who founded the Palestinian Medical Relief Society and is a political leader (you might hear him on NPR for instance as an articulate voice of reason), Dr. Mahmoud Suheil, the psychiatrist who is the head of the center, and a man from the European Union who spoke at a Birzeit Heritage festival we attended a few days ago. We all stand for a bout of patriotic music, the cameras roll, and the conference officially begins.

Today is the annual UN International Day in Support of Victims of Torture. The EU speaker talks about how torture is abhorrent, against moral and ethical values, "it destroys the victim and dehumanizes the torturer, and undermines the state that tolerates it. Torture is also a crime under international human rights law and unlike many other human rights, there are no exceptions or no justifications to make the unacceptable, acceptable." He notes that, "these are easy words, the real question is how to combat torture effectively."

He suggests that torture has to be addressed at different levels that include legal regulations where torture is prohibited by law and mechanisms need to be in place to make sure this is applied. It is also critical to have transparency, bringing to light behaviors at police stations and other places of detention. He asserts that civil society has a role to play here; this work requires public awareness of what torture does to people; this is a constant task, human rights values need to be frequently stated and restated.

In 2013, President Abbas decreed a prohibition on torture and in April 2014 Palestine ratified the UN convention against torture. (The US and Israel signed decades ago for what it is worth.) He notes these are important developments, but more needs to happen as Palestinian civil society has regularly reported the use of torture by its own security forces as well as by Israeli forces. He notes that the European Union has regularly criticized Israel regarding the conditions under which Palestinian prisoners are held and the use of administrative detention; he congratulates the treatment center and its partners that "deal on a daily basis with some of the darkest aspects of human experience." I wonder where is the voice of the United States at an important conference like this?

The next series of speakers are talking in Arabic and their main points revolve around the destructive Israeli practices of child arrests, the killing of young children, and the rearresting of prisoners who were freed in previous deals. There is then a long presentation on Palestinian and international rules, laws, contracts, etc., the bad things that have happened, the need for respect for women's rights, the illegal torture of Palestinians in Palestinian prisons and appalling Israeli policies and house demolitions.

This is all a bit overwhelming. I am looking through the conference literature and learn that the Treatment and Rehabilitation Center was founded in 1997 to defend human rights, to build a society free from torture through community awareness and education. Their tasks focus on: violence against prisoners, the wounded, families of martyrs, victims of the Apartheid Wall, road blocks, settler attacks, etc. They also offer treatment and support to victims and their families and focus on therapy and rehabilitation, medical and psychological. I am puzzled as someone appears to be setting up an electric piano on the stage.

A woman talks of transitional justice, the need to create official strategies to identify torture, to fix societies that are suffering, and to compensate victims. For victims, the torturer needs to be punished and the victim compensated. She notes that with the ongoing history of torture, this will lead to a loss of trust between individuals and society. She acknowledges that the divisions between Fatah and Hamas have created many victims and many people have been hurt.

After apologies to all the people who were unable to get to the conference due to the heightened delays and blocks at checkpoints, it is apparently time for the entertainment. A singing group from An-Najah University in Nablus, two women in gorgeous embroidered Palestinian dresses and one man playing the thing that looked like an electric piano but clearly is something else, pour their hearts into the music, giving voice and feeling to a society filled with pain and joy. This is all pretty extraordinary.

The second part of the conference is focused on treatment for prisoners and their families, "who are not sick, but suffering." They talk about men released from prison after over ten years who have never seen a smart phone, have had years of solitary confinement, physical, and psychological suffering, whose families were not allowed to visit. "But what about the feeling about the father, thinking about his kids, what has happened to them, what kind of treatment they can do to support them. They are suffering from beating, abused, not eating or inedible food. Some have abdominal pains due to bad food and no exercise and that makes it worse. The air is stagnant, six people in a room, health worsens."

The Center is doing awareness campaigns about the torture prisoners are facing, they have branches in places like Nablus, Jenin, and Ramallah, they offer outreach, go to the homes of the prisoners and families, talk to them; many do not have money to go to the center. The staff also uses psychotherapy, i.e., cognitive behavioral therapy; the Center sends staff to Norway to practice and learn to do therapy. Their group includes a psychiatrist and psychologists; they discuss each case and plan treatment, possible medications, psychotherapy, etc. The main goal is to make the victim feel better so he/she can go back to a normal routine and return to society.

The speaker gives a poignant example: one person spent thirteen years in prison, his oldest child was five and now he is eighteen, "So he will not feel like the father, lost that feeling. The child is used to the absence of the father, he, [the father], is not used to being ignored and not asked and is shocked, so he feels like a piece of furniture. He is not asked to participate in family as they are used to being without him."

When the psychiatrist determines that the released prisoner is ready, he or she is offered professional rehabilitation: the prisoners are paid a monthly income and offered courses to be able to work in their desired field, "so they will be productive in building a future, they want to become productive." Specialists follow the prisoner and evaluate the results and adjust the treatment program. The speaker is intelligent and articulate, the audience nods in agreement, and I have a sense that this is a group of sincere, decent professionals honestly working to better the lives of victims and their difficult society.

"The wife of the prisoner, she is the hero, but in the shadow. She is fighting alone to raise the kids, work, so the center is trying to offer the wife work options, i.e., sewing in a salon, which is in her home, so her kids are close, she can care for the kids and have an income while the husband is in prison."

There are more presentations about the legalities and international laws and the groups that monitor conditions. There are human rights committees that write reports in cooperation with organizations like Physicians for Human Rights Israel, "track all the kinds of violations and torture, in order to find the truth, and follow those reports to see more details, in front of government to take action. The torturer should know that he is going to be punished and is not protected."

Another speaker notes that in the news recently, "there is an increase of family fights that result in killing, so violence has increased in Palestine, girls are being raped. So the laws must be followed, the killer needs to be punished, otherwise the family takes justice in their own hands and this is dangerous."

There is more discussion about the deaths of Palestinians in Israeli prisons due to inappropriate medical care, the lack of punishment or accountability, the current prisoner hunger strike, the fact that Israeli violations are allowed because they are in power, the possible forced feeding legislation. "It is the worst occupation in history. It is not impossible emotionally to hope for Palestinian society without torture."

"Even any kind of reporting to Israeli institutions leads to nowhere. So it is time to do it ourselves by legal means."

Another speaker clearly is more agitated. He talks about the continued cases of torture by Palestinians in Palestinian jails. Of the havoc in Israeli jails and the need to use international committees and the media. "If the torturer is not punished, the Palestinian can track them down using international organizations and other countries and laws. Using the law we can find those murdered in Israeli prisons, those who abuse prisoners, and try to stop this. During interrogation they torture them until they die." He describes "Israel [as] a country of killing, torture, destruction, but we are strong and it is our turn to act, to make the laws and the policy." I can sense his outrage, voice rising in anger and frustration. He ends with the three kidnapped Israeli settlers and the difference in the international response when Palestinians are the victims. "When Israeli kills our children or rearrests prisoners, this is war, it is our right to ask for help through media as well."

The last speaker (before more singing) is a freed prisoner. I brace myself for some horrific litany of pain and suffering, the conference has already felt quite overwhelming and my professional boundaries are fraying. The young man begins by reading from the Quran; he explains, "One can face many difficulties, but if there is a huge trauma those who are patient, Allah promises them with heaven."

mulokhiya (Jew's mallow) that gets concocted into this great green soup with rice, and a field of wheat; much has been passed down through the generations.

The living rooms of these houses have big-screen TVs and often some totally discordant American cowboy movie with Arabic subtitles or an overly dramatic soap opera from Saudi Arabia playing in the background. It is stunningly hot and periodically someone talks about the four feet of snow that fell last winter and paralyzed the village. The land is hilly with single homes here and there; throw in some goat herds and minarets and if you keep looking you can see the Dead Sea and the purple hills of Jordan. It is all pretty spectacular.

This is the kind of family that warmly welcomes me into their home, the mother has prepared a ginormous meal of extraordinarily good food which is made of rice and chicken and stuffed grape leaves and stuffed zucchini, and yogurt and spices to die for; everyone is behaving as if I have not eaten in days.

We retire to a living room filled with stuffed chairs and stuffed people, and after more sitting and smiling and Sprite and Coca Cola, I take out my origami directions and a hundred sheets of colored paper. Shortly thereafter, there is a whole collection of family members of all ages and all levels of education making boxes and struggling over cranes and helping the kids get the creases right. This goes on for an hour and there is so much laughter and good fun; it is just a simple pleasure and feels so good in some primordial, mostly nonverbal human way.

My host then suggests that the family watch my documentary on the Nakba, *Voices Across the Divide*, and I wonder how that will play, a documentary produced by a secular Jewish woman for a US audience sharing the Palestinian story in a room full of devout Muslims (is this chutzpah or foolishness?) And so we talk and talk and I say they have to be honest with me. Everyone wants to see it and so they invite over more relatives and soon everyone is glued to the TV and we are not watching Bonanza.

I am a bit freaked out since they keep talking and I can't tell if this is good or bad, but it turns out this is a totally talkative enmeshed family and they are just having a big group experience; they recognize the two college girls holding the Boycott, Divestment, Sanctions sign towards the end of the film and of course the village of Beit Ummar over the hill; they are debating the different family names, who knew? When the documentary ends, I hold my breath, and then the father speaks and says the film is an excellent portrayal of the Palestinian experience and then everyone chimes in and we have this amazing discussion about all of their stories and the making of the film and the American Jewish community and Zionism, and Islam, etc., etc. As you may imagine, this is a pretty stunning, cross-cultural experience and I am so relieved; I feel embraced and welcomed despite my clear differentness. (I am given a bed in a room by myself and the entire family sleeps on long cushions on the floor in the living room.) Perhaps I need more tea and how about some nuts?

So why am I telling you this story? When you hear a news report, these are the "they," the "Muslim other," the "Palestinian militants near Hebron," the faceless families that are being terrorized by Israeli soldiers every night since the three boys (or settlers, or soldiers, or who knows what or all of the above) disappeared. The day after the disappearance (I will call it a kidnapping when I know that is what it was and, FYI, I am not asking Netanyahu for the real story), The Islamic Center and School for Boys next door was ransacked by the Israeli soldiers and the imam was detained for a few hours and then released. Years ago, his two brothers were "martyred"; one was in a militant group and died in a gun fight when the house was crushed with him in it and the other was killed as "collateral damage."

After our movie night and the sunset over Kiryat Arba, as we prepare for bed, I am informed that the Israeli Defense Forces have attacked the town, they are at all the entries and have started going house to house. The village has a Facebook page which is suddenly the focus of everyone's attention. Someone reports that three to four buses of fully armed soldiers are walking through the town, some take control of one house and put a sniper on the roof. TV news is talking about an IDF attack on Rafah, the southern border of Gaza. The electricity flickers on and off, why? The family is anxiously awake until the middle of the night, tracking the soldiers on Facebook and on a local radio program. The father finally goes to the mosque to pray when the muezzin calls at four a.m. (yes I am awake dissecting every sound), and then he comes home and goes to sleep. I learn that like many Palestinian men, he has been arrested twice and was in administrative detention for two months and released without any charges. He has obvious reasons to be anxious; he is a Palestinian male while Muslim, which is an arrest category in itself. No arrests are made here during the night, but everyone's nerves are a bit shattered and no one sleeps well. The youngest son is curled across his mattress and is in a deep stupor. I wonder how this all impacts him and his sense of safety, his belief in his parents' ability to protect him. The press is reporting hundreds of arrests, many more injured (collateral damage?), and a steady number of killings. Hamas members (including legislators) are clearly targeted.

Earlier, we passed one of the big "Bring Back Our Boys" signs; it hits me that this is supposed to resonate with the violent kidnapping of girls in Nigeria. I try to imagine a society where that slogan would mean all of our boys, not only the three snatched last week but the thousands of mostly boys and young men lost in Israeli detention centers without parents or lawyers or the legal and human rights protections of any decent society. And then there are all those boys who have lost their humanity, breaking into houses night after night, terrorizing families, turning into frightened, dehumanized monsters. And I realize, we need to bring them back as well.

In the Container

The bus station in Bani Nayim is hot, humid, and thick with exhaust fumes from idling vehicles that have seen better days in the seat and shock absorber department. The *service* has to fill with passengers before it leaves, and we are in a holding pattern. I am sitting next to a young woman wearing a hijab with sparkly threads, a long coat, long sleeves, and leggings. I cannot imagine how hot she feels cradling an infant and trying to keep a one-year-old in his seat. As she negotiates the crying baby and the discreet breast-feeding and attempts to pour mango juice into a bottle while it drips over the infant's plump thighs, I feel like we are mothers everywhere and it is time to mobilize for the tasks at hand. Chocolate wafers appear magically from my bag and the little boy stares at me with large brown eyes; he never blinks, ever.

I am wheezing from all the dust and pollution and marveling at what passes for advertising in the local markets. While most of the signs are in Arabic, I am mystified by a clothing store called, "White Woman," another "Lady Chic," the "Golf Plastic Industrial Company," "Four Seasons Furniture." Do they have four seasons here? There is clearly a lot lost in translation, which seems to be a metaphor for much that is happening in these parts.

We jolt by fields of vineyards and then there is a lush green vineyard that is surrounded by a wire fence and coils of barbed wire. It is the only fortified field I see and it is owned by a Jewish settler who has bought this land and comes, armed with military guards, to harvest his grapes. This is another metaphor.

My understanding is that there is some Israeli law/directive that mandates the use of seatbelts in the occupied territories but that Palestinians view this as another oppressive Israeli directive, rather than some really good advice, so I watch the on-off seat belt dance as we drive, a quiet (self-defeating?) act of resistance. I have not seen any car seats for children, so the mother buckles in her toddler, more as an attempt to restrain him in the back seat than to prevent injury in case of a sudden swerve. The much too loose belt soon comes off and she wraps her arm tightly around him, trusting herself more than those Israeli laws. He turns a bag of pretzels upside down and we are both back in mothering mode. A honey-toned woman's voice croons on the radio, I can pick out the word "Allah" but remain mostly lost in translation again.

We pass mountains of watermelon, car skeletons piled in junk yards like corpses, and overflowing garbage bins and soon find ourselves zigzagging up and down the Container Road, a vertiginous highway built specially for Palestinians that takes travelers miles out of their way, keeping that area "clean" for settlers. (see language: racism, entitlement, and fear) The *service* slows to a halt as we approach a massive traffic jam at the Container Checkpoint. Passengers get off and the driver asks me to move forward. I cannot tell if this is part of the checkpoint strategy. White American lady nearer to front? I decide to check the time and see what happens. It is a useful distraction and keeps me from total aggravation.

then we will just be in search of another bathroom. This is a delicate balance. The driver (bless him) finally turns on the air conditioning.

We head north(ish), this being the occupied West Bank, pass the now famous to anyone paying attention town of Nabi Saleh (see the *New York Times* article) where I joined internationals and villagers in 2012 on a Friday afternoon and watched the town's youth chant the words of Martin Luther King and Gandhi, throw stones, and run like crazy, while Israeli youth (in full military gear) shot an amazing amount of tear gas and rubber bullets. The Friday ritual of resistance still continues. We pass Halamish, the nearby Jewish settlement that is busy stealing land and water from the folks in Nabi Saleh, who having been living there for centuries. But that's another story.

Soon we arrive in the small village of Aboud, surrounded by settlements; the population is half Muslim and half Christian. This fact interests me. To my surprise, my new friend lives alone in a large U-shaped house with more rooms than she can fill, a large TV, and a pleasant kitchen. The windows are all closed and she has sprayed against mosquitos, so the smell of pesticide hangs heavy. Her enduring-the-heat strategy involves strategically opening and closing different shades and windows, sitting on porches on opposite sides of the house, and, when all else fails, turning on the fan, which I do since I seem to be having a permanent hot flash. The walls are scattered with crosses and virgins and saints and various homages to her beloved mother and father and a cast of cousins. She turns on the music and the Beatles blasts through the house, "It's been a hard day's night and I've been working like a dog..." She thinks that a salty yogurt drink will revive me and heads toward the kitchen to prepare her version of chicken and rice.

Over the course of the next twenty-four hours, I learn a lot. My friend loves Frank Sinatra. She loves to dance, and in a previous life she wore miniskirts and worked like a demon for five years at a suburban hospital in the United States after training as a nurse in Britain, against her father's wishes. She and her extended family were all born in Aboud, she received her nursing diploma during the First Intifada, travelling on a Jordanian passport. She flew back home in the days when a Palestinian could fly into Tel Aviv airport, only to discover that everything had changed. She remembers telling a nasty Israeli official, "The pendulum will swing, and we will get it back." After an emotional reunion with relatives in Jerusalem, her father took her back to the village. She only had a three-month visa (important reminder: to be in her own home). When she saw the large Israeli flag at the entry to her village, the reality of occupation hit her like a jolt of lightening. She stayed five months, her visa expired, and through sheer luck and a lot of chutzpah, she ended up living with a group of nurses from the UK and working long shifts at the US hospital in the days when nurses wore crisp uniforms and probably smiled and said "Yes, doctor" a lot. It sounds like she really enjoyed herself and her freedom.

Her first love married someone else; ultimately she returned home, the responsible daughter, to care for her aging parents, and now she is in a most unusual situation; an aging, lonely Palestinian woman without any children, her swarm of relatives mostly lost to the diaspora. She once had a job offer at Hadassah Hospital in Jerusalem, but Netanyahu nixed that when he forbid employing staff from the West Bank. I feel her regret. "Being a single woman in the village is like being in prison." When she talks of her long dead mother, her eyes fill with tears. Her stories are peppered with feisty bravado, she tosses around quirky expressions like, "Okay Charlie!" and has had her share of taking wild chances, standing up to soldiers at checkpoints. "They control everything, they control the oxygen you breathe."

"Kids were throwing stones and the soldiers were beating a kid. [I said] 'What are you doing? You are a kid with a gun. He is a kid with a stone. Be a gentleman. Put the gun away. And if I catch you throwing stones again, you will hear from me.'"

Once she was interviewed on the street by CNN and asked what she thought of the Israeli withdrawal from Gaza. "So what. I will be happy when they pull out of East Jerusalem, end the settlements, [let the refugees back]! Every night she prays for peace and listens to *Voices of Peace*, a radio station located "somewhere in the Mediterranean." Obviously she prays a lot and whichever God is in charge of this place seems to be hard of hearing.

My new friend cannot believe I am Jewish and she cannot believe she has an actual Jew in her home, eating her chicken and her chopped up cucumbers and tomato. "The first Jew in Aboud!" she exclaims happily. (I guess the Israeli Defense Forces don't really count here.) Her voice gets a bit conspiratorial and she advises me not to mention this fact in the village. She is worried about her Muslim neighbors, "They are a bit fanatic." She seems to be in the some-of-my-best-friends-are Muslims camp, but I also sense a deep distrust. So much for peace, love, and understanding, united against the common enemy (private thought). She talks of an upsetting night when a large truck and ten jeeps arrived at midnight and as she peered out the window, she saw her Muslim neighbor, blindfolded, handcuffed, dragged into the truck by Israeli soldiers. She suggests that I tell people I'm Italian.

When the heat abates a bit, she takes me on a speed walking tour, stopping to schmooze with family and friends. She complains about the garbage thrown by ill behaved (read Muslim) teens and when I comment on how hot it must be for women in hijabs and long coats, she says, "They're used to it. It's their religion." The town has wide streets, two Christian neighborhoods and one Muslim, and from what I can gather, three functional churches, a mosque, and ancient church ruins. We only tour the Christian sector. Some of the walls have lovely religious murals and others harken back to a simpler time when people were out harvesting their crops and looked much happier. We pass donkeys and their babies, elegant homes with lush gardens, abandoned properties, the site of my American friend's former family home (his bedroom is now a driveway for an ancient yellow probably Dodge Dart). A young man gallops by, riding his horse bareback, tail flying freely.

She is very angry about the ongoing land and olive grove confiscations, the nearby Jewish settlements, and tells me the story of finding an IDF soldier asleep under a tree. Her friend walked up to the sleeping soldier and yelled, "We gave you the road. You have the beach in Tel Aviv in your bikini. Leave us alone." The soldier had a gun and started threatening her friend who yelled, "Go ahead, shoot me. I will die defending my land and you will be a murderer." These women are tough. We come to a premature end to the road, obstructed by a ten-foot tall pile of dirt and rocks, courtesy of the nearby settlers in their orange roofed houses. I ask my new friend if I can take her picture in front of this dirt wall and she says quickly, "No." She is too upset for photo ops.

We stop at a series of stone patios, friends and relations drinking tea, eating watermelon, smoking cigarettes, hugging children.

I feel like I am in an old French movie or maybe visiting Uncle Morris and Aunt Bessie in Queens, ordinary schlumpy folks, full of opinions and quarrels and family loyalty, eat, eat, *habibti*. The women dye their hair black/brown and have thin pencil eyebrows. One guy, an engineer with a couple of charming, engaging young daughters, lived in the Bay area for years but then felt he had to come back. He tells me warmly and honestly, he could not tolerate the diversity, the Mexicans, the Asians, the Blacks. "I am not racist but I want to be with my own people." He didn't like the rat race, enjoys the slower pace, wants more time with his wife and kids. "Have some more watermelon?"

The next morning we see more of the churches, including the Church of the Virgin Mary "Abudia," which dates back to the fourth century. In the hushed entry, the priest chanting melodiously in the sanctuary, my friend lights candles and prays. We watch Sunday school children play with a gigantic multicolored parachute and act out Jonah and the whale. (What do these landlocked kids know about oceans?) We pour through exquisite Aboudi embroidery. (I am trying to find something without God or Jesus and am thrilled to see "Home Sweet Home.") The tour of the friends and relatives continues and it is close to heartbreaking. A sweet widow caring for her emaciated dying mother in a dark bare room, the faint smell of urine, three children; her son is apprenticed to a blacksmith. Another woman's brother built a palatial estate and visits in the summer. His elderly demented sister sits in the front door, half dressed, camping out on the first floor. She presses candy into our hands when she realizes we are not staying. Another friend tends to her ill brother with severe multiple sclerosis and an angry personality, her face is tight with sorrow. She wants me to send a package of her homemade *za'atar* to my friend in America and asks that I tell him to call and tell him "to come home." Another white-haired woman on her way to church says to me, "You are better than my relatives. They never visit." This is a tough place to be old or sick or alone. I feel that the villagers who escaped to the diaspora are both a source of pride and resentment. Despite all of its natural beauty, the village has an air of stagnation and suffocation that comes with small places, no secrets, and not much in the way of prospects for big happiness.

The visit is sweetened by a stop at my friend's family home across from her place, where a relative (not sure who) lives with his (quietly depressed?) wife and three gorgeous, lively daughters. The children adore her and I can see that she loves and indulges them like a grandmother. "Very lovely," she beams.

There is only so much tea a person can take and it is time to return to Ramallah. My friend explains that the Ford driver's basic attitude (he will only leave when the vehicle is full) is "Why hurry? Aboud to Ramallah to Aboud. We are all in prison." My friend gives me one more piece of advice: "Okay Charlie, my dear," we should prepare for a lonely end of life. That is our fate.

I meet up with a thirty-something activist friend in Ramallah, and as we sip our mint lemonade and hide from the Ramadan fasting police, she talks about life choices; she is tired of being beaten and tasered; she is really worried about injury and death; she wants to stop smoking, to have babies, to live. How to do all of that in this very complicated place?

June 30, 2014

Zionist Doctors and Jewish Values

It is probably not a good idea to write a blog after two glasses of wine, particularly after three weeks of abstinence (except for that lovely Taybeh Beer), but sometimes drastic measures are needed. I have checked into a funky old hostel in Jaffa that was clearly a Palestinian home before everything happened and I am sitting in a café watching the flow of beautiful people: the hipsters and the yuppies and the old-lumpy-young-at-heart like me. The sidewalk restaurant spilling into the street feels like a cross between Soho and San Francisco; gentrification on steroids and delicately rolled cigarettes (have any of you gorgeous people ever heard of lung cancer?); a stream of beautiful millennials with tattoos and fancy dogs and partially shaved heads. I feel like I am back in the good old USA where our troops are off doing Allah-knows-what in Iraq, Afghanistan, Pakistan, etc., etc., and we are obliviously obsessing about our lattes.

After two weeks mostly in the West Bank, the women look pretty naked, there is more than enough cleavage and thigh, men are stroking their lady friends in overtly sexual ways, and I am taking a long, hard look at "Western norms." I order a shrimp and eggplant dish drenched in garlic and olive oil as a metaphoric culturally transitional meal. I must admit I have a strong urge to just get up and walk away without paying the overpriced bill, just charge it to the occupation I will say (this is my version of civil disobedience), but I don't. Most of the folks I have been sharing lives and hummus with cannot legally be here, let's not even mention their yearning for a little dip in that gorgeous Mediterranean water, waves cresting, stretches of white sand ("they" do like to swim you know)… and I have to admit I kind of got used to being called "*habibti*," and my Arabic pet name, "Alusi" (my spelling with apologies).

The day started in the Old City in the Austrian Hospice with a predictable conversation with two lovely, older, guilt-ridden Germans who talked about how hard it is to say anything critical of Israel because... (the HOLOCAUST) is literally screaming at our table between the German Rye and the *labneh*, and I am trying to introduce the concept that it is actually okay. In fact, as a Jewish American, I think that it is imperative; the Germans (after the unforgiveable horror) have done their share of breast-beating and reflection and reparations; as some famous Israeli wrote, The Holocaust is Over. They take my website enthusiastically and I assure them that my book was translated into German, though of course I have no idea what the actual title was, given the wild world of publishing.

Last night I tried to make small talk with my first-in-a-while Jewish Israeli cab driver. Me: "It's been really hot here." Him: "No it's not." Oh right, the people who do not know how to say I'm sorry. Unfortunately, this morning I was bullied while standing in line for my train ticket, got yelled at by some pretty girl at a counter at the central bus station in Jerusalem when I asked for directions, and got no reassurance from the bus driver that this was indeed #480 to Arlozoroff in Tel Aviv. When I finally worked up my crumpled courage to confirm my hopes about the bus, this blond something said abruptly, "Of course." On the bus, a bearded Orthodox Jewish father with a gentle demeanor and friendly smile debated with his two teenage sons, "How can we know *Hashem* when *Hashem* is unknowable, is everywhere?" We all have our psychopathologies, but really?

I spent the afternoon at an extraordinary organization called Physicians for Human Rights–Israel. Ran Cohen was somewhat more optimistic than usual. Although the Knesset is probably about to pass the force-feeding bill, the prisoners' hunger strike ended (resolution unclear), and this has taken a lot of energy. "We won the battle but lost the war." For the first time in history, "We got the Israeli Medical Association aboard and this is surprising. They were vocal and said clearly physicians do not do this and discussed this [force-feeding] as torture." The IMA was clear that force-feeding actually involves the cooperation of doctors and that they would not be able to protect them in a court or even at the International Hague. This change in attitude may be related to a new head of the medical ethics committee, Dr. Tami Karni, as well as intense international pressure. Ran was very excited to see the commitment on the part of the doctors, the understanding that medicine and doctors were being used as political tools. The new law that is being argued in the Knesset today states that each case of forced feeding will be brought to a civil regional court (like Tel Aviv), and then if it is allowed, a doctor may participate without risk of punishment. The Israeli government is framing this as a desire to save lives (not). On a TV program, when some big *macher* said that there will be no doctors willing to do forced feeding, the government's legal advisor replied, "We will find the Zionist doctors who are concerned of Israeli security." So much for Zionism. Framing is obviously the key. The United States does it, so why not Israel?

Last week, PHR–Israel had a big success when a committee (that had seemed hopeless) decided to take private health services outside of public hospitals. Until now, in public hospitals, there were private patients that doctors would see and charge, using the hospital facilities, thus creating a boutique type practice on the back of the public system. There was a long campaign against this and, "We succeeded, after it lost in the Supreme Court! This was a public campaign, seven million citizens will benefit with a more equal health care system, oriented towards the public," as well as bucking the Israeli trend towards privatization (as I say, learning the worst from the American health care system).

Another recent PHR–I success involves the citizenship law. Since 2003, Palestinians in the West Bank and Gaza who married Palestinians with Israeli citizenship were not allowed what is called family reunification, i.e., they could not get legal status to live in Israel with their spouse. The implication of this cruel bill is that one of the couple, usually the woman, is left with no status, either cannot live with her husband or more likely is here illegally. Their children born in Israel are Israeli citizens. This is reminiscent of the undocumented in the United States. At this point, since 2003, twenty to twenty-five thousand couples got married and did not get status for the spouse, who can be deported at any time, has no health care, cannot enter most bus stations, malls, or any place where racial profiling increases the risk of being asked for an ID.

They cannot drive legally, attend university, or obtain welfare benefits. After the NGOs in the human rights community took the battle to the Supreme Court and failed, PHR–I started a long campaign to promote social residency, which separates legal status from social rights. This allows people access to health care and welfare regardless of their status. The State of Israel will not give one new Palestinian citizenship due to the demographic war, but PHR argued that the Palestinians are here, they are not temporary, they are married to Israelis, and they are human. PHR became aware of this issue when they started seeing desperate Palestinian women in their Open Clinic. Now, with the Association for Civil Rights in Israel (ACRI) and Kayan (a Palestinian feminist organization), they have "a foot in the door"; they won a court case that allows spouses with permits but no status to register for health funds. This covers eight thousand families, "so this is beginning, from nothing to something is big." This work is part of PHR–I's advocacy for the right to health for all.

The refugee issue also keeps PHR busy. Since 2003, fifty thousand refugees or asylum seekers (or if you are Netanyahu, "infiltrators") have crossed the Egyptian Sinai into Israel, mostly from Sudan and Eritrea. Many of them (an estimated 25% of the Eritreans) were kidnapped, tortured, raped, or held for ransom in the Sinai by a Bedouin clan. The Israeli response, wrapped in the hysteria of the threat to the Jewish nature of the state by these disease carrying, Muslim criminal elements, was to build a fence along the border with Sinai, so new refugees are no longer entering and the border is sealed. Sound familiar?

They also built a detention center called Holot, which means Sands, where asylum seekers and refugees are sent without a trial or judicial review for an indefinite period of time. It is "open" in that they can step out into the desert, but they need to be there for three roll calls per day and from eleven p.m. to six a.m. It is an utterly miserable place. Two days ago, six hundred men defiantly marched to Egypt, stating they want to go someplace where they can move their lives forward. They were brutally arrested again and sent back to prison, all documented on video and PHR–I was there to help the sick, mostly suffering from dehydration and injuries related to the attack by the security forces. Ran explains that the Israeli government is working to make these people miserable and has actually sent a few hundred to Sudan where many are reported to be detained, in danger, tortured, or imprisoned. Thirteen families have reported their loved ones missing, imprisoned, or murdered. A few have been sent by plane to third countries, mostly Rwanda and Uganda; Israel has some unofficial agreement with these folks. In Rwanda, a few have been detained, as documented by the United Nations High Commissioner for Refugees.

At this point Ran notes, there are fifty thousand refugees here, this is not a demographic catastrophe. Israel is a first world country; it could be a model for refugee absorption, and it has done it before with one million Russians (many of whom were not Jewish, but at least they were white). Meanwhile, both Lebanon and Jordan are both faced with one million Syrian refugees, each with much fewer resources. The least the Israeli government should do is to investigate each person's refugee and asylum issues and protect them until it is safe for them to return. Ran notes ironically that the whole discussion about protecting the "Jewish nature of the state" really leaves out the nature of Jewish values; this is all about numbers. PHR is once again working on the separation of legal status from social rights and they have had some successes. In January 2014, the government adopted a plan to treat HIV-positive refugees and established a small mental health clinic for these deeply traumatized people, so there is a glimmer of recognition regarding the right of health, even for people who are African and poor and so desperate they will walk across deserts and endure unbearable suffering to come to a place that might provide work and opportunity.

PHR–I also focuses on the occupied territories, and Ran describes a report that will be published in a month investigating basic health indicators for Palestinians in the West Bank and Gaza and comparing them to Israelis. Let's just say that everything looks bad; even basic life expectancy is divergent by more than ten years, as well as maternal and infant mortality, availability of medications, clinicians, specialists, etc., etc. This gives PHR the opportunity to talk about responsibility and control; if the Israeli government controls the territories as the occupying force (which it is), then it is responsible for the health needs of the population under its control. Netanyahu brags that, "Israel saves lives of Palestinian children while Palestinians are kidnapping teenagers"; this is nonsense. The Palestinian Authority is paying for the care in Israel, and for decades, the Israeli government has prevented development and actually "dedeveloped" the Palestinian health care system as well as controlled and reduced access to the major East Jerusalem hospitals. The facts speak for themselves as we say.

And then there are all the other projects: "torture always an issue, the victims are refugees and prisoners." There is work on the freedom of movement of doctors and patients in the occupied territories, the Saturday mobile clinic as usual, the Tel Aviv open clinic and much efforts to educate Israeli students in universities on the right to health by taking them on tours of East Jerusalem, the Negev, Bedouin villages, south Tel Aviv, Lod, Ramle. Ran notes, "The students are more and more open to it, the problem was with faculty not wanting us to come and talk, but things are getting better."

How Do You Say Shalom in Tigrenya?

Ran takes me into the Open Clinic for some reality-based learning. The rooms are basic health center with shelves of paper charts and two volunteers engaged with their computers. The dress is casual shorts and tank tops, the waiting room rows of black plastic chairs. Today is appointments only with the specialist, so I will not be seeing the usual flood of humanity, the human refuse as Lady Liberty would say.

Ran explains that in Israel, much like the United States, if someone presents with a life-threatening emergency to a hospital, they must receive care. (Good!) But everything else, including things that are in the long term life threatening, like out of control diabetes, is turned away if the patient has no insurance. (Health care as a privilege not a right.) And of course long-term rehabilitation, mental health, and medical follow up for chronic disease are hindered by access, language, poverty, and culture. Since 1998, the Open Clinic has seen thirty-five thousand patients, and many travel from far to be seen. PHR used to serve mostly migrant workers (after Palestinians from the territories were no longer permitted to work in Israel and employees started importing low-level workers from

Thailand, the Philippines, and the rest of the Third World.) Now PHR is mostly seeing asylum seekers and these folks are different: their communities are weaker, their leaders are under arrest; they are usually not working and suffer from all the ills of poverty as well as trauma and displacement. They are alive often because they are basically physically resilient young men. While much of the medications are donated and thus free to the patients, they often need shekels to get home, to eat. They are a more desperate population than the migrant workers. The clinicians are seeing more diabetes and hypertension, there are three thousand volunteers, but eight hundred or so are really active in the organization doing regular clinics.

The Open Clinic sees five thousand patients a year, "less patients but bigger problems than before," and includes general medicine, ob-gyn, pediatrics, and mental health. I sit down with the clinic coordinator, a feisty, dedicated young woman, former engineer, masters in international relations, and now a paid employee. Her job is to negotiate for the patients, to find the least costly, most possible appointments for specialists, labs, hospital procedures, surgery, and cancer therapy. Working with Assaf, a social care organization, they address medical as well as social issues like homelessness. She also is involved with the United Nations High Commission for Refugees (UNHCR) and helps refugees resettle in countries like Sweden, Denmark, or Norway, obtain citizenship and then medical care for severe chronic illnesses. I try to imagine fleeing something horrific in Sudan, running/hiding/walking across the Sinai, detention in Holot, some terrifying disease in a strange country, and then you end up in a place where everyone is blond, there is no sunlight half the time, winters are really cold, and the language is beyond comprehension. And you are sick and alone? This is staggering; the coordinator admits to many sleepless nights and desperate phone calls.

She talks about how the clinic is seeing many young patients with kidney failure and diabetes, maybe a consequence of toxic pesticide use, of Africans dying of AIDS in Israel in 2014, "This is ridiculous." And then in 2010, Sister Azezet, who volunteers at the clinic, noticed many pregnant women coming in asking for late-term abortions with unusual injuries and trauma. The Sister interviewed 1,300 women and discovered the rape and torture camps, the human trafficking in the Sinai, and brought this to international attention. "No one asked, what happened to you?" This is health care in its broadest social context.

The law in Israel now states that if an employer hires a migrant worker, they have to pay for health insurance. But when the employee gets sick, they get fired, and poof, no insurance. So the Open Clinic sees many Eritreans (they now have an interpreter), as well as migrant workers from the Philippines, China, and India. And then there are the folks from Nigeria, the Congo, Ivory Coast, and Guinea who have overstayed their work permits and live in the shadows, at risk for deportation at any time. Add to that a small number of Russians who arrived with the big migration but are not recognized as Jews and thus have no health insurance (really? Insurance for Jews only?) and the Palestinian women from the territories who married Palestinian men with Israeli citizenship and are unable to obtain legal status.

PHR is doing advocacy work on behalf of the asylum seekers now detained in Holot; they have gone to the Supreme Court applying for release from the center, stressing the illegality of detaining these men. She notes that public opinion is definitely against the refugees, who have been defined by Israeli government mind-makers as "infiltrators"; PHR is accused of supporting criminals, rapists, and disease carrying Africans, the scary, faceless, black other. "It is hard to humanize them."

The first woman the coordinator sees today is a fifty-five-year-old Filipino woman who has been in Israel for eleven years, has had no contact with her family during this time, speaks fluent Hebrew, and has recently had surgery for metastatic uterine cancer. She needs further treatment and the coordinator and I understand that she will most likely die alone and unhappy in Israel. I look at the pack of Marlboros next to the computer and the jumbo size bottle of Coke; this is burnout kind of work and the coordinator pours her heart into each case. The next patient, an Eritrean woman with a four-year-old son, also speaks Hebrew fluently, has a mass in her neck, brings lab results, and gets sent off to an ENT doctor. She is followed by an Eritrean man who speaks sort of English, has back pain, and is unable to work, now is dizzy. She asks him to come back tomorrow for the general doctor. I suggest we check his blood pressure and it is significantly elevated.

I then join the gastroenterology specialist; he is a good-hearted soul who is more in the classic doctor mode. He assesses each patient to see if there is anything life threatening or GI and does not sink his time into the vast psychosocial morass that is probably the source of much of the medical complaints. The first patient surprises me, a friendly, well-organized African American woman from Kansas City, Missouri, with lists and notes, who made *aliyah* with her family three years ago and is now living in Ashkelon, awaiting citizenship and health insurance. She has multiple medical problems, including a life threatening liver disease, and her granddaughter whose name is Aliyah is having her Bat Mitzvah in a week. "Can I drink wine for the blessing?" I would love to know the rest of her story!

She is followed by a series of Sudanese and Eritrean men with various levels of disease, lots of stress, experiences in the Holot detention camp, working or out of work, worrying about deportation, "I am not guilty, why keep me there?" Some speak Hebrew or a variant of English or Tigrenya. They are all thin, frightened, obviously depressed and sometimes angry; their eyes give them away. They are trying to negotiate a system that they do not understand, a language they do not speak, and a country that wants them to go away. The doctor does the best he can given the limited resources, the lack of communication between institutions, the need to beg and borrow to get medications, testing, results. No one is happy and I am haunted by the pained expressions and sorrow framing these difficult interactions. They say a society is only as strong as its weakest link and this link is clearly broken.

July 1, 2014

Airport *Hasbara*

The talk on the cab radio is all about the murder of the three set-tler teens, their bodies were found. I am too disconnected to know the awful details, but I recognize the outraged voices and the words Hamas and Philistini over and over. A great sadness and fear settles over me. I worry about my Palestinian friends and feel for the mothers of the dead boys and tremble at what wave of rage Netanyahu will unleash now. I suspect he will use this catastrophe to make a big attempt to destroy Hamas and eliminate the unity government, but that is a private speculation.

The airport feels remarkably normal; as Jonathan Cook noted last week, there are no more security attack lines and I feel less under siege. One female security guard asks me if I received any gifts in Israel and I brain scan the contents of my bags and decide to say, "Yes."

"What?"

"Embroidery."

"Embroidery?"

"You know, handicrafts."

"Where from?"

"Jerusalem"

"From whom?"

My tired mind freezes, what would be a reasonable answer? Why did I say yes? In that split second, the security officer goes on the offensive.

"You do not know her name?" Is she really accusing me of accepting a gift from a stranger (something really dangerous like an embroidered wall hanging that says "Welcome to our home"), or is the tone and aggressiveness just cultural or both. I come up with a safe and reasonable friend with an Italian name and American citizenship. My bags are tagged, I check my fellow travelers' bags and they have the same tags as me. Either we are all in trouble or we are all okay. I sail through the security check; it fascinates me that liquids, water bottles, and shoes are not a threat here. Does anyone know what they are doing? A repeating video reassures us that the baggage screening in Ben Gurion Airport is the most modern, high tech in the world so no worries. We have everything under control. Passport control is a piece of cake; apparently I am not in their system, as it should be. After all, I have not done anything illegal.

There is always a major photo exhibit on the long ramp into the duty free zone and food court and this year it is on civil aviation. I study the framing and language, after all, this is Israel's final chance at *hasbara* (propaganda messaging) for all the happy tourists going home to spread the word about the miracles of Zionism.

As would be expected, the tone is heroic, nationalistic, and full of struggle and victory: "Hundred years after the first airplane touched the ground of the Promised Land, the Israeli Airports Authority makes revolution in the aviation world..." My quirky brain asks, "Promised Land" for whom exactly? It all started with a French aviator landing on a Tel Aviv Beach in 1913. There are frequent references to "'Eretz Yisrael' (Israel)"; again the actual translation would be the Land of Israel and the real name of the place at that time was inconveniently Palestine.

The makers of the exhibit understand the vast arc of history: "Evolution of the civil aviation in the 1930s didn't skip the Jewish population in 'Eretz Yisrael' (Israel). The Jewish national institutions' leaders fully understood the economic and security importance of the Jewish aviation for the future of the Jewish population." It is interesting that Palestine Airways was started in 1937 in what is referred to as "Lydda (Lod)," an unexpected nod to an Arab city now renamed and transformed. On the other hand, the messaging is clearly reflective of Zionist mythology building, "From its first days, the civil aviation in Israel was interlinked with the Zionist ethos and symbolized the technological progress." Of note, the early aviation clubs and flight schools in the 1930s were linked to the Haganah, a Jewish paramilitary organization, and to the Irgun, described as "The national military organization of the land of Israel." No mention of who they were fighting and the political assumptions of Jewish exceptionalism and violence undergirding the effort (wrong story).

There are archival photos of the Yemenite "Operation Magic Carpet" in 1949 and the Ethiopian Jews arriving with the "Moses Operation" from 1984 to 1985, flown from refugee camps in Sudan through Belgium to Israel. A document reviews the many clandestine flights from Yemen and Iraq from 1948 to 1952, from the Soviet Union from the 1970s to 1990s, and then the Ethiopians in the 1980s. The language fascinates me: the references to some mythical Arabic tale or biblical exodus. This was all demographics disguised as rescue, from what I can see. We need more Jews; the Holocaust decimated the preferred type, so now we will take Arabs and Blacks and even not exactly Jewish Russians. Am I being too cynical?

The archival photos reveal pilots who are all white Ashkenazi men, and then there is the Arab worker with some kind of machine, labeled "aerospace industry production worker," probably Yemenite. The racial and class differences are already apparent if you care to look.

The airplanes were called the "Iron Birds" and the pilots "the Knights of the Skies"; again the messaging is all strength and heroism that leads to the establishment of modern Israeli companies, now celebrating ten years after the construction of this current snazzy terminal "One of the most modern security inspection systems in the world." Translation: Israel will keep you safe.

Passengers are left with messaging that is full of nostalgia without all the messy details, reflections on past struggles and victories to come. Tell the world the glorious story of Israel as you head towards the glittering Duty Free zone. There is no occupation, no Apache helicopters in Gaza, no dead settler children, no Palestinian resistance or for that matter, Palestinian anything. As I said, with my binocular vision, a great sadness and fear settles over me. Obviously, I didn't get the message.

July 7, 2014

Footnote

I have been home almost a week; my brain is nearly in Eastern Standard Time, though my nights are filled with hours of anxiety and wakefulness, and I am indulging in my usual addiction to the news, mainstream and otherwise. Commenters talk about the current upsurge in violence, "after a period of relative calm," clearly they have not been paying much attention, have they? The American citizen who was brutally beaten by Israeli security is under house arrest (for what crime exactly?) and a reporter uses the expression, "apparent excessive use of force" by the Israelis. Has he seen the videos proliferating on the internet, they are not that subtle. On NPR, some talking head reports on the lack of progress between, "the two governments, Israel and Palestine," as if we are talking about two equal states that just need to calm their extremists down and settle their squabbles. The horrific murder of the three settler boys from Hebron is mentioned without context; there is apparently no ugly occupation, no crushing siege of Gaza, no angry extremists that even Hamas may not be able to control anymore, no regular Israeli incursions, arrests, murders, home demolitions, no fanatic, racist Jews screaming "Death to the Arabs." It strikes me as suspicious that the murderers of the settler boys have not been clearly identified and located in a region crawling with collaborators and security apparatus. Something is clearly amiss. Liberal Israeli Jews may squirm and condemn their fascistic, xenophobic brethren, but these folks have been allowed to flourish under every government and in fact, I fear, are the product of a country that has taken Zionism and Jewish exceptionalism and privilege way beyond the boundaries of human conscience.

Interestingly, Netanyahu sent a condolence call to the dead Palestinian child's family, but as we know, he does not have a good track record when it comes to justice. I think for the first time in my life, I read a report in the *Boston Globe* that actually uses the words attributed to the Israel defense minister to describe the revenge killers who burned Mohammed Abu Khdeir to death as "Jewish terrorists." His cousin, Tariq Abu Khdeir, visiting from Tampa, is in the news a lot. It seems that beating a Palestinian with American citizenship is hard to hide. But, of course, then there was Rachel Corrie. Forgive my cynicism.

I stop by a local liquor store that is owned by a Palestinian family from Taybeh just to say hello, to express some sympathy, when a customer with red hair and an Irish face overhears the conversation and remarks, "Wow. You've been there!" He asks where the Palestinian owner is from, and the guy says, vaguely, a small village near Jerusalem. Obviously being Palestinian from the occupied territories may not be good for business in Brookline. The customer's face lights up and he says, "You guys sure make great music." It takes me a moment to realize that he thinks this little village is in Israel, probably does not even know that there is a place called Palestine, and is basically clueless. When he leaves, we restart our conversation about "extremists on all sides" and the possibility that this is the beginning of the Third Intifada.

One of the medical students on the exchange program from Al Quds University is staying with me while doing rotations at a variety of Harvard hospitals (and fasting all day for Ramadan). He loves to walk and explore the neighborhoods, has already joined a gym, and is very focused on shopping; he has a long list of relatives and needs a gift for each of them from the great bastion of capitalism and discount outlet stores. He was at the hospital when a (presumably highly educated) resident said, "We have some other students from Israel." He calmly replied, "I am from Palestine." He met the Israelis and reassures me, "They are okay."

Meanwhile, all the parties are behaving according to the script. Israeli forces are attacking Gaza, Palestinian militants are shelling Sderot, Palestinian youth are rioting in East Jerusalem and Hebron, Jewish gangs are causing havoc everywhere. The unity government between Fatah and Hamas is just about dead and the Palestinian Authority, which most often works in collaboration with the Israeli occupation forces, is its usual, less-than-productive self. Israel remains a powerful, energetic, gorgeous, ugly, out-of-control, profoundly racist state and American Jews mostly line up to support "our homeland." I note that several major temples in the Boston area are sponsoring memorial services for the dead *"Yeshivabochas"* and I wonder, when will we have the decency and wisdom to mourn for all of our children and the political will to stop the uncritical support of Israeli policy and the blindness to the suffering, resistance, and resilience of our Palestinian brothers and sisters. All of our futures depend on this.